Table of Contents

5   Preface: Embarking on a Sacred Investigation
7   Introduction: Unraveling the Mystery of the 3,000

Part I: The Historical Foundations

9   Chapter 1: The Puzzle of the First Believers
15 Chapter 2: The Ancient Keepers of the Covenant
21 Chapter 3: The Maccabean Revolt and the Great Expulsion
26 Chapter 4: Clash of Beliefs - Sadducees, Pharisees, and Essenes

Part II: The Messianic Connection

32 Chapter 5: The Calendar Clash - Zadokite Solar vs. Pharisee Lunar
37 Chapter 6: The Two Messiahs - Prophecy Fulfilled
42 Chapter 7: John the Baptist - The Priestly Messiah
49 Chapter 8: Yeshua - The Kingly Messiah

Part III: The Essene Legacy

53 Chapter 9: The Essenes' Qumran Community - Secrets of the Scrolls
59 Chapter 10: The Damascus Document - Zadokite Exile Unveiled
62 Chapter 11: Paul and the Way - From Persecutor to Disciple
67 Chapter 12: The War Scroll - Sons of Light vs. Sons of Darkness
71 Chapter 13: The Holy Spirit - Essene Belief and the Fire of Acts 2
75 Chapter 14: Restoration and the Elijah Connection
80 Chapter 15: From Sinai to Qumran to Today - The Restoration

Part IV: Broader Impacts and Modern Relevance

84 Chapter 16: The Essenes' Influence on Early Christianity
89 Chapter 17: The Essene Call Today - Restoring the Covenant
93 Chapter 18: The Role of Women in Essene Communities

Part V: New Discoveries and End-Time Revelations

 98 Chapter 19: The Zadok Calendar Revealed
 106   Chapter 20: The Gold Book Discovery in Arabia
 115 Chapter 21: End-Time Ties and Modern Implications
 122 Conclusion: The Legacy Unveiled and the Quest Continues

Supplementary Materials

 125 Appendix A: Timeline, Glossary, and Scriptural References
 135 Appendix B: The Ineffable Name of Yehováh
 151 Bibliography
 157 Bonus Content

Patrick McGuire and Dr. Miles Jones, '23 Saudi Arabia Real Mt. Sinai Expedition

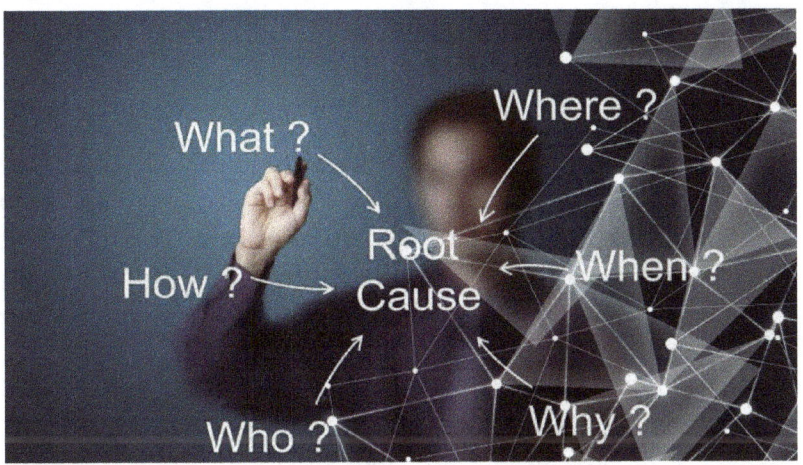

Preface: Embarking on a Sacred Investigation

As I sit down to write this preface on a crisp morning in Kerrville, Texas, I am struck by the timelessness of the story about to unfold. This book is not just a recounting of history; it is a detective story, a spiritual quest to uncover the roots of the 3000 believers who, on that transformative Shavuot in Acts 2, embraced the Holy Spirit's outpouring. My journey began with a simple question: Who were these individuals, and why were they ready when others were not? What I discovered was a trail leading back through the Essenes, the Zadokite priesthood, and the very covenant established at Sinai—a path illuminated by ancient scrolls, biblical texts, and conversations with scholars like Eddie Chumney who is a research expert on the Qumran community.

This investigation has been both personal and communal. Inspired by insights from my research for my book; *Sons of Zion vs Sons of Greece*, I've sifted through the ancient Hebrew Gospel texts, wrestled with calendar disputes, and traced the high priests from Aaron to the Maccabean upheaval. The result is a narrative that bridges past and present, inviting readers to join me in exploring how these events shape our faith today.

This book is for those who love a good mystery, who seek to understand the deeper currents of scripture, and who yearn to live out the covenant in a modern world.

The appendix—featuring a timeline of high priests, a glossary of terms, and a wealth of scriptural references—serves as an essential guide, offering tools to delve deeper into the evidence. Together with the timeline of priestly succession from Exodus 28:1 to 1 Maccabees 1:10-15, these resources ground our exploration in historical and biblical reality. My hope is that this work not only answers the question of the 3,000's identity but also ignites a passion to carry forward their legacy of faith, readiness, and restoration.

To my readers, I extend an invitation: step into this story with an open heart and a curious mind. The evidence is ample—from the solar calendar's precision to the Essenes' battle against corruption—and the conclusion awaits. As we stand at this moment in the 21st century, let's embark together on this sacred investigation, seeking the truth that connects us to those 3,000 souls and the God who guided them.

I have worked hard to moderate my normally scholarly prose into a storyline easier to read - without losing any archaeological details of the hunt. Patrick McGuire, my co-author, has been a major part of making that happen.

In this book I will be using the Hebrew name of God - Yehovah, and title Yeshua the Messiah (Jesus Christ) and Holy Spirit instead of the old English Holy Ghost. All English scripture references are taken from the King James Version (KJV). Verses taken from the Hebrew Text Version will be noted as (HTV), which are from the Heberew Gospels Translation Project by the Benai Emunah Institute (BEI), which has a mission to translate the ancient Hebrew manuscripts of the entire New Testament that have recently been recovered, as well as individual books. The BEI international team has the goal of completing the Hebrew Gospels in 2026.

                         - Dr. Miles R. Jones

Introduction: Unraveling the Mystery of the 3000

Picture this: Jerusalem, 31 AD, buzzing with pilgrims for the feast of Shavuot, or Pentecost. A group of believers gathers, and suddenly, the air crackles with divine energy—a sound like a mighty wind, tongues of fire, and voices speaking in languages they shouldn't know. Peter stands up and preaches about Yeshua's resurrection and the Holy Spirit, and 3000 people respond, getting baptized and joining a radical new movement called "the Way" (Acts 2:1-41). Who were these 3000? Why, out of thousands of pilgrams, did only they answer the call? This book sets out to solve that mystery, and trust me, it's a trail that twists through ancient prophecies, hidden scrolls, and a forgotten priesthood, leading to a truth that resonates even today.

This isn't just a history lesson—it's a detective story, piecing together clues from the Hebrew Bible, the Dead Sea Scrolls, and the Hebrew Gospels. Our journey starts at Mount Sinai, where God forged a covenant and appointed Aaron, the Levite priest, and his sons to guard it (the Zadokite priests are their direct decendents). We'll follow their path through exile after the Maccabean revolt, to the Essenes who kept their flame alive in the deserts of Qumran and "Damascus." These Essenes, with their solar calendar, belief in two Messiahs—John the Baptist and Yeshua—and hope for the Holy Spirit, are the key to unlocking why the 3000 were ready for Acts 2. Along the way, we'll uncover a Hasmonean cover-up that tried to erase their legacy, only for their scrolls to survive, dug up almost 2000 years later declaring truths about a New Covenant!

This book traces the Zadokites' influence from Sinai to the early church. We'll explore prophecies like Zechariah's "two anointed ones" (Zechariah 4:14), Malachi's Elijah promise (Malachi 4:5-6), and Isaiah's "way of holiness" (Isaiah 35:8), all pointing to John and Yeshua as the Messiahs the Essenes expected. We'll see how their *War Scroll* framed a cosmic battle, how Paul's conversion tied to their teachings, and how their faith shapes our call to restoration today.

Each chapter builds the case that the 3,000 were Essenes, primed by their Zadokite heritage to recognize God's move in Acts 2. From their solar calendar ensuring they were in Jerusalem at the right time, to their communal living mirroring the early church, the clues are compelling. But this isn't just about the past—it's a challenge for us to reclaim the pure faith of Sinai, free from human traditions, as we await the Messiah's return.

So, grab a touch, because we're diving into caves, unrolling scrolls, and following a trail from Sinai to Jerusalem to today. The 3000's story isn't just history—it's a call to join the "Sons of Light" in a battle for God's truth. Let's get started!

Chapter 1: The Puzzle of the First Believers

Okay, let me tell you something right off the bat—this is the kind of mystery that grabs you by the collar and doesn't let go. I've spent years digging through ancient scrolls, chasing down forgotten histories, and piecing together clues about the roots of our faith. As a historian and expert in ancient Hebrew texts, I've seen things that'll make your jaw drop. But nothing, and I mean *nothing*, has hit me quite like the question we're about to tackle: Who were the first 3000 believers in Acts chapter 2? You know, the ones who heard Peter testify at Shavuot—Pentecost to most folks—and got baptized in one fell swoop? We've been told that's the birth of the Christian church. But hold on a second. What if I told you they weren't starting something brand new? What if they were reclaiming a faith so ancient it stretches back to Mount Sinai itself?

This book is my journey to crack that mystery wide open. It's not just a history lesson; it's a detective story, like following a treasure map through the sands of time. We're going to hunt for clues in hidden records, lost priesthoods, and a seismic shift in history that got buried under layers of dust. I'll lean on my talks with experts on the Zadokite priesthood, my own research into Hebrew manuscripts, and insights from research for my book

Sons of Zion vs Sons of Greece. Everything here is grounded in real evidence, but I'm writing it so all can follow along—no fancy talk, just the straight scoop. By the time we're done, you'll see why figuring out who these first 3000 were changes how we understand the Messiah, the early believers, and even the calendar we use today. So, buckle up; we're diving into the greatest unsolved puzzle of the New Testament.

The Scene at Shavuot: A Game-Changing Moment

Let's set the stage. Jerusalem is buzzing like a beehive. The festival of Shavuot, also called Pentecost by the Greeks, is in full swing. Jews from all over the Mid-East and beyond—Parthians, Medes, Elamites, Syrians, you name it—have packed the city to celebrate. This isn't just any holiday; Shavuot commemorates God giving the Torah to Moses at Sinai. Picture thousands of pilgrims, dusty from travel, crowding the streets, offering sacrifices at the Temple, and praying for a move of God. Then, in Acts 2, something wild happens. The Holy Spirit comes down like a rushing wind, tongues of fire appear, and the apostles start speaking in languages they've never learned. Peter stands up, preaches about Yeshua the Messiah, and says, "Repent, and be baptized every one of you in the name of Yeshua the Messiah (Jesus Christ) for the remission of sins, and you shall receive the gift of the Holy Spirit" (Acts 2:38). The result?

> **"Then they that gladly received his word were baptized: and the same day there were added unto them about three thousand souls"** (Acts 2:41).

Three thousand people. That's no small number. It's not like Peter was handing out free falafel to draw a crowd. These folks were moved, convicted, ready to change their lives on the spot. But who were they? Were they just random Jews caught up in the moment? Or was something deeper going on? In all my years studying ancient texts, I've learned one thing: big moments like this don't happen by accident. There's a story behind those 3000, and it's a story most believers have never even questioned. Yehovah was plowing the ground for this event just as He had prepared for the entire ministry of His Son. He did not simply drop the Messiah off on a streetcorner in Jerusalem. He prepared the ground, the people, for what was to come. He called the Apostles just as He put His Holy Spirit and understanding into those New Covenant believers, the Essenes.

The Question Nobody Asks

Here's where it gets interesting. I sat down with Eddie Chumney, a researcher who's spent decades unraveling the Zadokite priesthood, and he hit me with something that stopped me in my tracks. In all his 50 years of research and speaking, and listening to every kind of Christian teaching out there, he'd never heard *anyone* ask:

Who were these 3000 Jewish believers?

It's like we've all just assumed they were a random bunch who got lucky hearing Peter's testimony. But that doesn't add up. Jerusalem was packed with maybe 100,000 people for Shavuot.

Why did only these 3000 respond? What made them different?

I started digging deeper, and the clues pointed to a group most folks overlook: the Essenes. You've probably heard of them because of the Dead Sea Scrolls, those ancient manuscripts found in caves near Qumran, off the northwest shores of the Dead Sea. But back then, the Essenes weren't just some desert hermits. They were a major Jewish sect, one of the big three according to the historian Josephus. The other two? The Pharisees and the Sadducees. To figure out who the first 3000 were, we need to look at these groups and see which one fits the bill.

The Three Sects: A Quick Rundown

Josephus, writing in the first century, laid it out plain: there were three main Jewish groups in Yeshua's time. The Pharisees were the ancestors of today's Orthodox Jews. They believed in the Torah but added a ton of oral traditions, claiming they came straight from Moses at Sinai. They said these rules—called the *"Oral Torah"*—were just as sacred as the written Bible, maybe even more so. They didn't think much about the Holy Spirit, and they clashed with Yeshua over their extra laws added to the Torah. Think of them as the religious rule-makers, sticklers for their traditions.

The Sadducees? They were a different breed. They ran the Temple, but they were cozy with the Greeks and later the Romans. They only accepted the first five books of the Bible—the Torah—and rejected ideas like resurrection or angels. They were more about power than faith, and Yeshua called them out for it. In the Hebrew Text Version (HTV) of Matthew, he doesn't even call them priests, just "scribes" or "soferim" (Matthew 23:2). That's a dig—they didn't deserve the title of righteous priests. Although they were scribes they left no writings.

Then you've got the Essenes. These folks were different. They lived in places like Qumran, following a pure form of the Torah without all the extra "oral" rules. They believed in the Holy Spirit, resurrection, and two Messiahs—one priestly, one kingly. They called themselves "the Way" and "Sons of Light," fighting against the "Sons of Darkness," which included the corrupt Temple leaders. Their writings, like the Dead Sea Scrolls, are full of prophecies about the New Covenant! Sound familiar? That's the kind of faith that lines up with what happened in Acts 2.

Clue #1: The Holy Spirit Connection

Here's the first big clue: the outpouring of the Holy Spirit. In Acts 2, the Spirit comes in a big way—wind, a bright light, fire, diverse languages. Peter quotes Joel: "And it shall come to pass in the last days, saith God, I will pour out of my Spirit upon all flesh" (Acts 2:17). Now, think about it. The Pharisees didn't emphasize the Holy Spirit; they leaned on their Oral Torah for guidance. The Sadducees? They barely believed in anything supernatural. But the Essenes? They were all about the Spirit guiding them to truth. Their scrolls talk about God's Spirit cleansing and leading the faithful.

The Essene Zadokites were required to do a three-year apprenticeship before officially entering the movement, "In order for the Holy Spirit to teach them the true meaning of Scripture!" (from the Dead Sea Scrolls – Manual of Discipline) When the Spirit fell at Shavuot, it was like a neon sign pointing to the Essenes!

"They were Jewish people that became believers, they are the Hebraic roots of faith in the Messiah"

Those 3,000 Jewish believers at Acts chapter two, which happened following the crucifixion of Yeshua, they became the roots of our faith in Yeshua, and because they were Jewish people that became believers, they are the Hebraic roots of faith in Messiah. These weren't just any Jews—they were the Hebrew roots of what we call Christianity, but back then, it was the Messianic faith. And the Essenes, tied to the Zadokite priests, were the ones ready to receive that message.

The Zadokite Connection: A Hidden Thread

Now, let's talk about the Zadokites. These weren't just any priests. They trace back to Aaron, Moses' brother, chosen by God at Sinai to lead worship. By the time of King David, Zadok was the high priest, overseeing the building of the First Temple. For over a thousand years, the Zadokites kept the true calendar, recorded Israel's history, and guarded the faith. The word "Zadok" means "righteous," and they were called *tzadikim*—the righteous ones.

But something happened around 167 BC, during the Maccabean revolt. The Hasmoneans, who fought off the Greeks, also kicked the Zadokites out of the Temple. They wanted control, so they installed their own priests and burned the Zadokite records to cover their tracks. This was a clash between Hebrew purity and Greek corruption. The last Zadok high priest, Onias III, was assassinated! Under great oppression the Zadokites fled Jerusalem. The Zadokites didn't disappear, though. They fled to places like Qumran and Damascus, keeping their traditions alive. The Essenes were their followers, holding fast to the true Zadok priesthood and Zadok calendar.

This is huge, folks. The Zadokites weren't just a footnote; they were the backbone of the true Messianic faith! And when Yeshua came, the Essenes were waiting for him—and for a priestly Messiah, too, like John the Baptist. Zechariah 4:14 talks about "the two anointed ones, that stand by the Lord of the whole earth." The Dead Sea Scrolls, such as 4Q76 Malachi 3:1-2 "The Messenger and the Master… Who can resist them when they come!", as well as other books of the time such as The Testament of the Twelve Patriarchs, confirm that they expected two Messiahs. Could the 3000 have been these folks, ready for both Yeshua and John?

Why It Matters: The Roots of Our Faith

You might be thinking, "Okay, Dr. Jones, this is cool history, but why does it matter?" Here's why: those 3000 weren't starting a new religion called Christianity. They were Jews, steeped in the Torah, reclaiming the faith of their fathers. Acts 2:44-45 says they "had all things common" and sold their possessions to share with the needy. That's straight out of the Essene playbook—they lived communally, sharing everything. The Pharisees and Sadducees? They were more about power and wealth.

This mystery isn't just about who these people were; it's about the roots of our faith. The 3000 were Essenes, tied to the Zadokites. Therefore the early "church" was a Messianic movement, not a break from Judaism but a restoration of it. Each sect had a different calendar or way to count the Omer (days) to Shavuot, which explains why only the 3000 were there when the Spirit fell. The way they counted time holds the key to unlocking this puzzle.

Chapter 2: The Ancient Keepers of the Covenant

We're stepping into the foundation of our mystery, like uncovering the cornerstone of a sacred temple buried in time. The Zadokite priesthood isn't just a footnote in history—it's the bedrock of the covenant that leads us straight to the 3000 believers in Acts 2. Their story begins at Mount Sinai, where God forged a divine contract with Israel, and stretches to the reigns of David and Solomon, where the Zadokites shone as guardians of holiness. We'll explore how these priests preserved God's plan, setting the stage for the Essenes and the early church. This is no dusty tale—it's the root of why those 3000 were ready for Peter's inspired words. Let's dig in!

Sinai: The Covenant's Sacred Blueprint

It is 1446 BC, the Israelites are camped at the foot of Mount Sinai, fresh from Egypt's chains, their hearts still racing from the Red Sea's parting and manna falling from heaven. Here, God delivers the Torah—a divine constitution for His chosen people. In Exodus 19:5-6, He declares, "If you will obey my voice indeed, and keep my covenant, then you shall be a peculiar treasure unto me... a kingdom of priests, and a holy nation." Central to this covenant is the priesthood, tasked with bridging God and Israel.

Exodus 28:1 sets the stage: "And take thou unto thee Aaron thy brother, and his sons, that he may minister unto me in the priest's office." Aaron, from the tribe of Levi, and his sons are consecrated to oversee the Tabernacle, a portable sanctuary where God's presence dwells. Leviticus 8, describes their anointing—oil poured, blood sprinkled, garments donned—a ritual marking them as holy mediators. Their duties? Offer sacrifices, teach the Torah, and maintain the sacred calendar of feasts like Passover and Shavuot (Leviticus 23:2).

The Zadokites trace directly back to Aaron through Eleazar, his son.

The Zadokites' role at Sinai laid the foundation for the Essenes, who saw themselves as heirs to this covenant, preserving it against corruption. The Zadok priesthood traces back to Levi and is a continuation of the Levitical priesthood through Aaron and his descendants – Eleazar, Phineas then down the direct

Chapter 2: The Zadokite Priesthood's Origins

line to Zadok, the high priest of King David and Solomon. The name Tzadik – means righteous – as in the first righteous priest of God Most High mentioned in Scripture, Melchi-Zedek (Melchizedek), which can be translated as King of the Righteous - the righteous ones or the righteous priests.

This wasn't a casual job. Numbers 18:5-7 charges the priests with guarding the sanctuary, ensuring no "stranger" defiles it, on penalty of death. They were timekeepers, too, using a 364-day solar calendar, rooted in the Book of Enoch and Jubilees, to align feasts with the Crerator's rhythm of the seasons (Genesis 1:14). This calendar, as we'll see in Chapter 5, is key evidence why the 3000 where there for Shavuot on the exact date the Acts 2 outpouring of the Holy Spirit happened in Jerusalem.

The Wilderness and Judges: A Priesthood Tested

For 40 years in the wilderness, Aaron's descendants, his son Eleazar and Eleazar's son Phineas, led worship in the Tabernacle, teaching Israel to distinguish "between holy and unholy" (Leviticus 10:10). The Exodus was full of challenges. The Israelites fell into idolatry and defied Yehovah, causing great plague to fall upon them, but Aaron and Eleazar stopped the plague. As a result, Yehovah set it to be a "memorial unto the children of Israel, that no one not of the seed of Aaron come near... before Yehovah!" (Numbers 16:40).

Yet the original priestly line of Levi, Aaron, Eleazar and Phineas held firm, guiding the Israelites throughout their history of triumph and tragedy. To Phineas, and his seed, was given "the covenant of an everlasting priesthood." (Numbers 25:11-13) because he had stood against those slipping back into the worship of Ba'al Peor.

Then Zadok arose, a direct descendant of Eleazar and Phineas (1st Chronicles 6:3-8). His name from *tzadik*, meaning "righteous," wasn't just symbolic—it defined his legacy. The Zadokites emerged as the faithful remnant, committed to God's original design. Their steadfastness during Israel's turbulent years set them apart, preparing them for a pivotal role under King David and Solomon. The Zadokites were like a lighthouse in a storm, keeping the covenant's flame alive when others faltered.

Yehovah bestowed upon Zadok, and his sons, the care of His eternal Temple. "These priests, the sons of Zadok, from among the sons of Levi, who come near to Yehovah to minister unto Him." (Ezekiel 40:46). This was definitely the everlasting priesthood of Yehovah, anointed by Him over and over again throughout the history of Israel.

David's Reign: Zadok's Rise to Prominence

Fast-forward to ~1000 BC, and King David, a man after God's heart (1 Samuel 13:14), transforms Israel. He conquers Jerusalem, making it the spiritual and political capital, and plans a Temple to house the Ark of the Covenant. Zadok steps into the spotlight. In 2 Samuel 8:17, we read, "And Zadok the son of Ahitub, and Ahimelech the son of Abiathar, were the priests." Zadok's loyalty shines during Absalom's rebellion, when he risks his life to carry the Ark, supporting David's rightful claim (2 Samuel 15:24-29).

David organized the priesthood into 24 courses (1 Chronicles 24:1-19), ensuring round-the-clock Temple service. Zadok led these efforts, overseeing sacrifices, music, and Torah teaching. His role wasn't just ceremonial; he was a spiritual anchor, ensuring worship aligned with God's commands. The Damascus Document later calls the Essenes "sons of Zadok" (CD, 3:21), linking their mission to this era. 16 of the priestly courses were designated to the "sons of Zadok," including the 8th course the course of Abbiah, to which Zachariah later belonged and his son John (the Baptist) would inherit his place as priest – so these two were clearly "sons of Zadok." Are you getting the connection here? David's vision for a unified Israel, with Zadok at its spiritual helm, prefigures the Essenes' belief in the New Covenant, which the 3,000 in Acts 2 inherited.

Solomon's Temple: The Zadokite Golden Age

When Solomon initiates the First Temple around 957 BC, it is Zadok the high priest who would have supervised the building of the Temple. the Zadokites reach their peak. In 1 Chronicles 29:22, "they anointed... Zadok to be high priest", cementing his authority. The Temple, a marvel of cedar and gold (1 Kings 6:18-22), becomes the center of Israel's worship. Zadok and his sons orchestrate daily sacrifices, major feasts, and the Day of Atonement, when the high priest (Zadok) enters the Holy of Holies (Leviticus 16). They also write the histories of the Israelites, preserve sacred records of the past already written, including genealogies and prophecies - ensuring the covenant's continuity.

Ezekiel 44:15-16 praises them: "The priests, the Levites, the sons of Zadok, that kept the charge of my sanctuary when the children of Israel went astray... they shall come near to me to minister." Their duties extended beyond rituals. They were educators, teaching Israel to discern "holy and profane" (Ezekiel 44:23), and judges, settling disputes per Deuteronomy 17:8-9. The Zadokites were God's librarians, guarding the Torah, calendar, and prophecies without adding man-made rules.

The Zadokites used the solar calendar, with 12 months of 30 days plus four seasonal markers, totaling 364 days. This ensured feasts like Shavuot fell on fixed dates, unlike the later lunar calendar. This precision, rooted in Genesis 1:14's "lights... for seasons", was a Zadokite hallmark, preserved by the Essenes. It explains why the 3000 were in Jerusalem on the right day for Acts 2's outpouring of the Holy Spirit.

As your historical detective let me note: it seems that throughout history there have always been in use both the solar and the lunar calendars. Even today we use the Gregorian solar calendar for dating history, but many also use the Aviv (lunar) calendar from Israel for dating the feast days. Both have been used, officially, in the Jerusalem Temple at different times. The Zadok calendar was replaced by the Greek lunar calendar, originally from Babylon, when the Zadok priesthood was replaced. It was one of the major reasons the Greeks orchestrated the takeover of the Temple.

They wanted to Hellenize the Jews.
Make all the world Greek!

We might call it the Tammuz calendar, since one of the months is named Tammuz, you know, the son of the Babylonia Sun god Nimrod Ba'al and his wife, the Queen of Heaven – Semiramus - also known as Astaroth, Baalat, Isis, Aostra to name a few. Many of the month names in the lunar calendar reflect aspects of paganism. One might wonder if Yehovah approves.

Cultural and Spiritual Significance

The Zadokites weren't just priests; they were cultural anchors. Their role as teachers shaped Israel's identity, ensuring every tribe knew the Torah's laws, from dietary rules to moral codes (Leviticus 11, 19). Their calendar-keeping unified the nation around God's *moedim* (appointed times), fostering a rhythm of worship that countered pagan influences. In *Sons of Zion vs Sons of Greece*, I argue this solar calendar resisted Babylonian corruption, a fight the Essenes continued.

Their genealogical records, preserved in 1st Chronicles, protected the priestly line's purity, a concern later echoed in the Essenes' scrolls (1QS, 5:2). This obsession with lineage tied to the prophecy of a priestly Messiah, fulfilled by John the Baptist (Chapter 7). The Zadokites' faithfulness, even through exile, inspired the Essenes to see themselves as the "sons of Zadok," guarding the covenant against Hasmonean betrayal (Chapter 3).

The Acts 2 Connection: A Legacy Preserved

Why does this matter for our mystery? The 3,000 in Acts 2 weren't random converts; they were Essenes, heirs of the Zadokite covenant. Their presence at Shavuot, on the solar calendar's date, aligned with the Spirit's outpouring (Acts 2:4). Peter's testimony, quoting Joel about the Holy Spirit (Acts 2:17), resonated with their Zadokite-rooted hope for restoration in the New Covenant, as Ezekiel 36:27 promised: "I will put my spirit within you." Their communal living (Acts 2:44-45) mirrored the Zadokites' emphasis on holiness and unity.

The Zadokites' story sets the stage for the Essenes, who carried their calendar, purity, and Messianic belief into Yeshua's time. The Hasmonean cover-up, burning Zadokite records, tried to erase this legacy, but the Essenes preserved it in their scrolls, paving the way for the 3,000. This is just the beginning—our next clue takes us to the Maccabean revolt, where the Zadokites faced their greatest test.

Chapter 3: The Maccabean Revolt and the Great Expulsion

We've been on quite the trail so far. In Chapter 1, we cracked open the puzzle of those 3,000 believers in Acts 2, and established they are followers of a forbidden and forgotten Zadok priesthood. Then, in Chapter 2, we traced the Zadokites back to their roots at Mount Sinai, through their glory days under David and Solomon as God's faithful keepers of the covenant. They were the righteous ones of Yehovah, guarding the Torah, and the eternal Temple, and the holy calendar without corruption. But now, the plot thickens. We're heading into a dark chapter of history around 167 BC—the Maccabean revolt. This wasn't just a heroic fight against Greek invaders; it was a power grab that booted the Zadokites out of the Temple, shattered their influence, and led to a massive cover-up by destroying their historical records.

This "sea change," as I call it, set the stage for everything that followed, including why there are "four centuries of silence" in the historical record of Israel leading up to the Messiah, and why those 3,000 were ready for the Messiah. Let's follow the clues and uncover how the perpetrators rewrote history to hide their tracks.

I've pieced this together from ancient sources and my own research into Hebrew texts. It was a major historical sea change in the history of Israel, which affects us all since it is a shared religious origin. It's like finding a hidden room in an old mansion—full of secrets that explain the ghosts haunting the house. By the end of this chapter, you'll see how this expulsion of the Zadok priesthood created the Essenes as we know them, preserving the Zadokite flame in the wilderness. And that flame? It ignited at Shavuot in Acts 2.

The Greek Shadow: Setting the Stage for Revolt

To understand the Maccabean mess, we need to rewind to the 4th century BC. Alexander the Great sweeps through the Middle East, conquering everything, including Judea. After he dies, his empire splits, and the Seleucid Greeks take over Syria and Judea. These Greeks weren't content with just ruling; they wanted to Hellenize everyone—turn Jews into mini-Greeks with their gods, gyms, and sexual proclivities. By the time Antiochus IV Epiphanes grabs the throne in 175 BC, things get ugly. He bans Hebrew practices, desecrates the Temple by sacrificing a pig on the altar, and sets up a statue of Zeus. It's straight out of Daniel 11:31: "And they shall pollute the sanctuary of strength, and shall take away the daily sacrifice, and they shall place the abomination that makes desolate." The Jews are furious. A priest named Mattathias and his sons, the Hasmoneans (later called Maccabees, meaning "hammer"), lead a guerrilla revolt starting in 167 BC. They fight back, reclaim villages, and eventually retake Jerusalem in 164 BC. Hanukkah celebrates that victory and the rededication of the Temple. Sounds heroic, right? But here's the twist: the Maccabees didn't stop at beating the Greeks. Eventually, within two generations, they turned on their own— the Zadokite priests.

The Expulsion: A Power Grab in Disguise

The Zadokites had been high priests for over a thousand years, from Sinai to the Second Temple. They had massive support; after all, they were the "righteous priesthood" God Himself established. But the Hasmoneans? They were from a different priestly family, not Zadok's line. Once they won the war, they wanted total control. Around 152 BC, Jonathan Maccabee appoints himself high priest, even though he's not a Zadokite. His brother Simon follows suit in 140 BC, making it official. The true Zadokites were kicked out, exiled, their authority stripped.

Why? Power. The Hasmoneans blended the role of king and priest, something God never intended. This was indeed a "sea change!" The Maccabees took over the temple and kicked the Zadok priesthood out. The Jews never restored God's priestly system! The Zadokites had a vast following, you can imagine, after 1,300 years of being the righteous priesthood of Yehovah. The Zadokites fled all over the region—places like Qumran and

Damascus and Leontopolis in Egypt, and other parts of Arabia—taking their scrolls and traditions with them. In Judea they became known as the Essenes, waiting for God to restore justice while preserving the Tanakh and their New Covenant writings.

This expulsion wasn't peaceful. The last Zadok high priest Onias III was assassinated! Others were targeted. It was a coup, and it left a vacuum where the priesthood had been. the Hasmoneans knew they had to fill it. They upgraded the Sadducees to the priesthood. They had helped them militarily to gain the throne. The Sadducees were morally flexible and willing to bend to the powers that be whether Hasmonean, Herodian, Greek or Roman. They were put in charge of the Temple and kept that power for centuries. The Pharisees emerged around this time too, more orthodox, pushing their oral traditions of Torah as a new authority.

The Cover-Up: Burning the Evidence

Here's the smoking gun in our mystery: no records of this expulsion survive in mainstream Jewish history. Why? Because the winners burned them. Why is there no record of this? Their records were burned. The Zadok priests were in charge of keeping the records, the history of Israel. So if you're kicking them out, you're gonna destroy their records. It's the oldest trick in the book—erase the evidence to rewrite the story. The Zadok records contain both their authority and Israel's history

We only know about this from fragments: the Dead Sea Scrolls, like the Damascus Document, describe the Zadokites' exile to Damascus after being ousted. Josephus mentions the Essenes as one of the three major sects in Israel, but he doesn't spill the beans on the coup. The book of Maccabees? It is in Greek, from Alexandria, and it glorifies the Hellenized Hasmoneans while ignoring the Zadokite fallout. The history books are written by

Chapter 3: The Maccabean Revolt and Expulsion of Zadokites.

the conquerors, who skip the ugly parts. Their version becomes the official history as long as there is no other version to contest it. So, all other versions must be destroyed!

This cover-up had huge consequences! Ever since the Zadok priesthood ended - the high priesthood was up for sale. Herod the Great appointed and deposed high priests like changing socks. The true priestly line? Scattered and hidden, some in the desert of Qumran, preserving the pure faith. In the Hebrew Text Version of Matthew, Yeshua warns about false leaders: "The scribes and the Pharisees sit in Moses' seat" (Matthew 23:2)—Yeshua never calls the Sadducees priests- he always refers to them as scribes. That's a clue—they weren't Zadokites. Sadducees comes from the name **Tzadikim** -righteous ones- but they were not of the Zadok line. They just stole the name to rebrand themselves. Clever, but it did not make them righteous.

Ties to the Mystery: From Expulsion to Essenes

Now, connect the dots to our 3000 believers. The expelled Zadokites didn't vanish; they formed communities like Qumran, calling themselves Essenes. They kept the solar calendar, believed in the Holy Spirit, and awaited two Messiahs. The Essenes were the followers of the Zadok priesthood. When the Spirit fell at Shavuot, it was on their calendar date, not the Hasmonean one. That's why only 3,000 responded—they were the ones gathered, ready for restoration. After their three-year apprentice-ship, they would gather at the Temple on the feast day of Shavuot in order to receive the benediction making them a member of the Essene community. Get this, they were expecting a baptism of water and the Holy Spirit!

This expulsion created a two-century rift. The Temple was corrupt, run by puppets. The high priesthood was for sale. The Temple had become a scam to fleece the righteous. The money went into the pockets of the priests, kings, and Greek or Roman overseers. Everyone got their cut. The Essenes? They were the remnant, the "Sons of Light" in their War Scroll, battling the "Sons of Darkness." John the Baptist, with his Zadokite roots, echoed this: "O generation of vipers, who hath warned you to flee from the wrath to come?" (Matthew 3:7).

The Lasting Impact: A Faith in Hiding

The Maccabean cover-up didn't just hide history; it shaped the future. Rabbinic Judaism rose from the Pharisees, ignoring the Zadokites. But the Essenes preserved the truth, influencing Yeshua and the early believers. This clash was between Zion's sons (Hebrew purity) and Greece's sons (corruption). The 3,000? They were heirs to that purity, responding to Peter's call because their hearts were primed by Zadokite teachings.

But here's the question nagging at me: If the Essenes were so different, how did their beliefs stack up against the Pharisees and Sadducees? And which group was truly ready for the Messiah? That's the showdown we'll tackle next. What if the key to unlocking Acts 2 lies in their core doctrines?

Chapter 4: Clash of Beliefs - Sadducees, Pharisees, and Essenes

Alright, folks, we're knee-deep in this mystery now, and it's time to roll up our sleeves and get to the heart of it. We've tracked the Zadokite priesthood from Sinai to their golden age under David and Solomon, only to see them kicked out during the Maccabean revolt, their records torched to hide the truth. Those exiled Zadokites became the Essenes, a group whose initiates comprised the first 3000 believers in Acts 2.

Keep in mind that the Essenes never once in the Dead Sea Scrolls called themselves "Essenes." It was historians like Josephus who laid that moniker on them. They referred to themselves as the "Sons of Zadok!" But why them? Why not the Pharisees or Sadducees, the other big players in Judea? To crack this case, we need to compare their beliefs head-to-head and see why these Zadokites were uniquely ready for Peter's inspiring invitation and the Holy Spirit's outpouring at Shavuot. This is like laying out the suspects' alibis in a detective story, and trust me, the Essenes' beliefs line up with Acts 2 like a key in a lock. Let's dive in. By the end, you'll see why the Essenes were the ones waiting for the Messiah—and why it matters for our faith today.

The Three Sects: A Snapshot of Judea's Spiritual Landscape

By the time Yeshua walked the earth, beginning his ministry in 30 AD, Judea was a spiritual battleground. The historian Josephus tells us there were three main Jewish sects: the Sadducees, the Pharisees, and the Essenes. Each had their own take on God, the Torah, and prophecy. Understanding their differences is like sorting through clues to figure out who was in the crowd when Peter preached in Acts 2:41, where "about three thousand souls" were baptized. Were they Sadducees, cozy with Roman power? Pharisees, obsessed with their rules? Or Essenes, the desert faithful? Let's break it down, starting with each group's core beliefs, and see who matches the facts in Acts.

The Sadducees: Power Over Faith

First up, the Sadducees. These were the elite, the ones running the Temple in Jerusalem. Think of them as the religious aristocrats, hobnobbing with the Romans and their Hasmonean predecessors. They were descendants of the priests who took over after the Zadokites were expelled, as we saw last chapter. But their beliefs? Pretty thin. They only accepted the first five books of the Bible—the Torah—and rejected anything about resurrection, angels, or the Holy Spirit. Josephus says they denied "the immortal duration of the soul, and the punishments and rewards in Hades" (*Antiquities*, Book 18, Chapter 1).

In the Hebrew Text Version of Matthew, Yeshua calls them out: "Woe unto you, scribes and Sadducees, hypocrites! for you shut up the kingdom of heaven against men" (Matthew 23:13). No resurrection, no spiritual gifts—sound like folks in need of a sermon about a risen Messiah and the Holy Spirit's fire? Not a chance. The Sadducees were more about keeping their power than seeking God's truth. When Peter preached about Yeshua rising from the dead and the Spirit pouring out, the Sadducees would've scoffed or walked away. They're out of the running for our 3000.

The Pharisees: Rules Over Spirit

Next, the Pharisees. These were the teachers of the law, the forerunners of today's Orthodox Judaism. They believed in the whole Hebrew Bible—Torah, Prophets, Writings—and added their Oral Torah, a set of traditions they claimed Moses received at Sinai. The Pharisees said the Oral Torah was given to Moses and passed down perfectly, but that's like a 3000-year game of telephone. It doesn't hold up. Their rules covered everything—how to wash hands, tie sandals, making more rules like a hedge around the Torah to protect it. They thought following these traditions made you righteous.

But here's the rub: the Pharisees downplayed the Holy Spirit. They believed righteousness came from studying and obeying *their* laws, not from divine guidance. In Matthew 5:17-18, Yeshua says, "Do not think - I came that I might breach the Torah - or the prophets. I came not that I might fulfill but rather that I might fill (the Torah) to overflowing, abundantly overflowing!" He's

Chapter 4: Comparing beliefs of Sadducees, Pharisees, and Essenes

challenging their additions, saying the written Torah does not need more Oral Torah laws. The Pharisees clashed with Yeshua constantly, calling him a lawbreaker for healing on the Sabbath, for example, because that was work which was prohibited on the Sabbath day (Matthew 12:10-14).

Would they have jumped at Peter's call to repent and receive the Spirit? Doubtful, that would dimish their claim to authority. Their focus was on rules, not spiritual renewal. Plus, their Greek lunar calendar, borrowed from Babylon, meant they would not even celebrate Shavuot on the same day as the Essenes. The Pharisees don't fit the Acts 2 crowd either.

The Essenes: Keepers of the Pure Faith

Now, the Essenes—here's where things get exciting. These folks lived apart, often in communities like Qumran, where the Dead Sea Scrolls were found. They were the spiritual heirs of the Zadokite priests, calling themselves "Sons of Zadok" in their scrolls (1QS, Community Rule). Unlike the Sadducees, they believed in resurrection, angels, and the Holy Spirit and the New Covenant. Unlike the Pharisees, they stuck to the written Torah, rejecting man-made traditions. To sum it up: the Essenes believed the Holy Spirit would guide them to all truth, and they were looking for two Messiahs—one priestly, one kingly.

Their scrolls, like the Damascus Document, begins by describing themselves as a remnant entering into the New Covenant in exile. They expected a "Teacher of Righteousness" to lead them and two Messiahs to restore Israel. Zechariah 4:14 mentions "the two anointed ones, that stand by the Lord of the whole earth", and the Dead Sea Scroll 4Q76 speaks of Malachi 3:1-2 to say, "And who can abide them when they come." That's plural—two Messiahs, not one. The Essenes saw John the Baptist (one of their own) as the priestly Messiah and, on that Shavuot in 31 AD, they recognized Yeshua as the kingly Messiah.

When Peter preached about the Spirit and Yeshua's resurrection, it was like lighting a match in a room full of dynamite for the Essenes. Acts 2:17 quotes Joel: "I will pour out of my Spirit upon all flesh." That's Essene language—spiritual renewal, not rule-following. Their belief in communal living also matches Acts 2:44-45: "And all that believed were together, and had all things common." The Essenes shared everything, unlike the wealth-hoarding Sadducees or rule-bound Pharisees.

Clue #2: The Essene Alignment with Acts 2

Here's the big clue that ties it together: the Essenes' beliefs match the Acts 2 scene perfectly. First, the Holy Spirit. The Dead Sea scrolls of the Essenes, like 1QS, describe God's Spirit cleansing the faithful and guiding them to truth. When the Spirit fell at Shavuot, it was exactly what they expected. **Second**, the resurrection. Peter's testimony hinges on Yeshua rising from the dead (Acts 2:24-32). The Sadducees would've walked out; the Pharisees might've debated. The Essenes? They believed in the resurrection and eternal life in heaven to come. They were nodding, not arguing, ready to sign up. They recognized their "Teacher of Righteous" who had been written about in their scrolls.

Third, their identity as "the Way" (Acts 9:2, 19:9, 19:23, 22:4, 24:14, 24:22). Acts calls the early believers "the Way," a term straight from the Essenes' scrolls, where they describe themselves as following "the Way of holiness" (Isaiah 35:8) and (Isaiah 40:3) "The voice of him that cries in the wilderness, Prepare you the Way of Yehovah." Isaiah 40:3 was the verse cited by the Essenes in the Dead Sea Scrolls that called them to create the monastery in Qumran, called the "Wilderness" by the Judeans.

It was their slogan, their marching orders, according to their writings. They went into the Wilderness to "prepare the Way of Yehovah" according to their own admission. The Essenes called themselves 'the Way' because they followed the pure Torah, guided by the Holy Spirit, waiting for the two Messiahs, the Teacher of Righteous (Yeshua) and his Priestly Harbinger (John). When Peter called for repentance and baptism, that they might be saved, the 3,000 Essene Zadokites saw it as their moment of salvation. It was what they had been preparing for all of their lives, for generations even. It is what they had been waiting for.

That moment, often called the "birth of Christianity," had arrived! To be real, it was the birth of the Messianic movement – they would not be called Christians until centuries later. In the Hebrew Gospel of Acts (11:26) it says,

they "were first called 'Messianics' in Antioch."

The Greek scribes later changed it to "Christians," after *Iesous Xristo* whom we have come to know as Jesus Christ, the very same as Yeshua the Messiah but in Greek.

The Calendar Connection: Timing Is Everything

There's another piece to this puzzle, and it's a doozy. The Essenes used the Zadokite solar calendar, 364 days, with fixed dates for feasts like Shavuot. The Pharisees used the Greek lunar calendar, which shifted dates yearly because it was determined, not by the Spring Equinox like the Zadok calendar, but rather by the observation of when the barley was ripe which varied from year to year. The Sadducees? They had a different method of "counting the Omer" the seven Sabbath days from Passover until Shavuot. As Scripture says, "When Shavuot **had fully come** in" (Acts 2:1) they were awaiting the final celebration, that of the Zadok calendar.

When the Spirit fell on Shavuot, it was the Essenes' date, not the Pharisees' or the Sadducees'" The 3000 there, were Essenes and their initiates - awaiting the profoundly meaningful experience of being anointed into "The Way," the Zadokite community of believers. They were in exactly the right place, the Temple at Jerusalem, at exactly the right time, guided by their Zadokite Hebraic roots.

Why It Matters: The True Roots of Acts 2

This comparison isn't just academic; it's a revelation. The 3000 weren't random Jews or a mix of sects. They were Essenes, primed by their Zadokite heritage to receive the Messiah's message. Their faith wasn't new; it was a return to the covenant God gave at Sinai! With one addition that is, they were dedicated New Covenant believers!

But here's the kicker: if the Essenes were on a different calendar, how did it shape their expectations? And what does it mean for the timing of Shavuot in Acts 2? That calendar clash is our next clue, and it's going to flip this mystery on its head. What if the way they counted time was the secret to why the Spirit fell when it did?

Chapter 5: The Calendar Clash - Zadokite Solar vs. Pharisee Lunar

Folks, we're zooming in on a clue that's like the ticking heart of our mystery, a clock that set the stage for the 3000 believers in Acts 2. We've traced the Zadokite priesthood from Sinai, their role under David and Solomon, and their exile after the Maccabean revolt, with the Essenes carrying their torch. The 3000, Essenes, were ready for Peter's sermon because of their deep covenant beliefs, and one key piece is their calendar. The conflict between the Zadokite solar calendar and the Pharisee lunar calendar wasn't just about picking dates—it was a battle over God's sacred time versus human invention. This clash explains why the 3,000 were in Jerusalem at the exact moment for Shavuot's miracle. Let's unpack the mechanics, scriptures, and insights to see why this calendar fight matters.

God's Time: The Zadokite Solar Calendar

Time isn't just a human tool; it's God's design for worship. Genesis 1:14 declares, "Let there be lights in the firmament of the heaven… for signs, and for seasons, and for days, and years." The Hebrew word for "seasons," *moedim*, means appointed times—God's holy days like Passover, Shavuot, and Sukkot. The Zadokite priests, tasked at Sinai (Leviticus 23:2), used a 364-day solar calendar to keep these feasts precise, aligning with creation's rhythm.

The solar calendar came from God through Enoch, preserved by the Zadokites. It kept the feasts fixed, unlike the lunar calendar's drift. The Calendrical Texts from Qumran (4Q320-321) detail this system: 12 months of 30 days, plus four days, called *Tekufahs* marking the turn of the seasons - the equinoxes and solstices - totaling 364 days. Divisible by seven, it ensured Sabbaths and feasts fell in a consistent cycle. For Shavuot, one counted 49 days from the day after the Sabbath following Passover (Leviticus 23:15- 16), this meant a fixed date, the 14th day of the third month. This precision, rooted in the *Book of Enoch* and *Jubilees*, was a Zadokite hallmark, preserved by the Essenes.

The solar calendar's structure reflected divine order. Each quarter of the year (91 days) included three months and one marker day, a *Tekufah* either an equinox or a solstice. *The Book of Jubilees* (6:23-38) declares this calendar was given to Noah, ensuring feasts like Shavuot, tied to the wheat harvest, stayed in season. This wasn't just practical—it was theological, signaling God's unchanging plan, as Psalm 89:34 says, "My covenant will I not break, nor alter the thing that is gone out of my lips." The Noah story from Genesis in the Dead Sea Scroll 4Q252 confirms the use of the Zadok calendar.

The Pharisee Lunar Calendar: A Babylonian Compromise

During the Babylonian exile (586–516 BC), many Jews had become habituated to the lunar calendar, based on Babylonian (p.31 PDF) astronomy, that calendar was also used by the Greeks. By the Hasmonean era (2nd century BC), the Pharisees embraced it, using 12 or 13 lunar cycles (lunar months) of 29–30 days, totaling ~354 days. To sync with the solar year, they added an intercalary month (Adar II) every three years, a human adjustment that shifted feast dates annually. The lunar calendar was a Babylonian import, not God's design. The Pharisees' Oral Torah justified it, but it broke the covenant's rhythm.

In Scripture there appear to be verses that support the lunar calendar and others that support the solar calendar indicating both were widely used at times. Both were used as the official Temple calendar during different periods. Because of this, it is confusing to answer the question, what calendar did the Hebrews use? Apparently both. The history of civilization tells us both solar and lunar calendars were used in ancient cultures. The Egyptians, along with the Babylonians, had figured out the solar calendar by the third millennium BC. It was far more precise than the lunar calendar but the lunar was far more useful for religious observance. People of antiquity did not have a calendar from the dollar store pinned to their kitchen wall. That was not needed with a lunar calendar, everyone can see when the moon is full, or when there is no moon... the moon festivals signal themselves.

This shift had spiritual consequences. Leviticus 23:4 commands, "These are the feasts of the Lord... which ye shall proclaim in their seasons." The lunar calendar's variability disrupted this. A 354-day

Chapter 5: The Calendar Conflict: Zadokite Solar vs. Pharisee Lunar Calendars

lunar year loses 11 days each year, and requires the addition of a 13th month every three years to get back into sync —feast days could shift by days sometimes even a week or more— struggling to align worship with observation of the ripeness of the harvests. The Sadducees, controlling the Temple, used the lunar calendar because their foreign masters demanded it, first the Greeks, then the Romans. The *Damascus Document* condemns this, noting those who "went astray" from God's calendar (CD, 3:14). *The Book of Jubilees* is even more adamant:

> "There will be those who assuredly make observations of the moon – how it disturbs the seasons and comes in from year to year 10 days too soon. For this reason the years will come... when they will disturb (the order) and make an abominable day the day of Testimony (Atonement) - and make an unclean day – a feast day. They will confound all the days, the holy with the unclean, and the unclean with the holy, for they will go wrong as to the months and sabbaths and feasts and Jubilees." (Jubilees 6:36-37)

Shavuot's Timing: The Key to Acts 2

The calendar clash is our big clue for Acts 2. Shavuot's date varied between systems. The Essenes' solar calendar fixed it, on a Sunday, 50 days after the Sabbath following Passover. The Pharisees' lunar calendar, however, could place it differently, often a week or two apart. Acts 2:1 says, "When the day of Pentecost was fully come," indicating there was more than one celebration. Why only 3,000 out of Jerusalem's thousands? The 3,000 were Essenes, celebrating Shavuot on the Zadok calendar date, ready and expecting the Holy Spirit's outpouring upon their initiation!

This wasn't just about timing—it was spiritual alignment. The Essenes, "Sons of Zadok" (1QS, 5:2), saw the solar calendar as part of their fight against corruption, as the *War Scroll* pits the Sons of Light against the Sons of Darkness (1QM, 1:1; Chapter 12). John the Baptist's preaching against the "vipers" (Matthew 3:7) echoed this, rejecting the lunar calendar's corruption. The 3000, gathered on the right day, experienced the Holy Spirit's annointing (Acts 2:4), fulfilling Ezekiel 36:27: "I will put my spirit within you!"

Cultural and Spiritual Divide

The calendar wasn't just a schedule—it defined identity. The Zadokites and Essenes saw the solar calendar as affirming God's covenant over time, resisting Babylonian pollution. The *Community Rule* (1QS, 10:1-8) emphasizes precise timing for prayers and feasts, reflecting their obsession with divine order. The Pharisees' lunar calendar, backed by their Oral Torah, symbolized to the Essenes a broader drift toward paganism. Yeshua opposed these "commandments of men" (Mark 7:7-9, HTV). The Hasmonean's adoption of the Greek lunar calendar, as Josephus notes (*Antiquities*, 18.1.3), submitted them to Greek, then Roman, authority - requiring them to remove the Zadok priesthood from the Temple. The Dead Sea Scrolls *Habakkuk Pesher (Commentary)* specifies that it was argument over the date of the Day of Atonement that was the catalyst leading to their ouster.

> **The Zadok calendar frames the year within the Spring and Fall Equinoxes, and the Summer and Winter Solstices - guaranteeing the seasons and the harvests will be aligned with the calendar.**

The lunar calendar's variability, it loses 11 days every year, disconnects feasts from their seasons if not corrected, weakening their significance. The 3,000 Essenes' presence at Shavuot, on the solar date, shows they followed the Zadok legacy, ready for the Spirit's confirmation of the covenant (Acts 2:17).

The Broader Implications

The calendar clash wasn't just logistical—it was a theological war. The Essenes' scrolls, like 4Q321, meticulously list feast dates, showing their commitment to God's *moedim*. Their rejection of the lunar calendar was part of their identity as the "remnant" (CD, 1:4), preserving Sinai's purity against Hasmonean manipulation. The early church's resistance to man-made traditions, as seen in Paul's warnings against "philosophy and vain deceit" (Colossians 2:8) was a reflection of their orthodox Essene origins.

For the 3000, their use of the Zadok solar calendar was an article of faith. It also ensured they were in Jerusalem when Peter preached (Acts 2:14- 36). Their communal living (Acts 2:44-45), communion and baptism reflected Essene practices, tying them to the Zadokite vision of a New Covenant. Today, as we'll see in Chapter 17, movements reviving the solar calendar echo this call to align with God's calendar.

Later in Chapter 19, we'll dive into this ancient mystery, exploring how God's calendar, etched in the heavens, led the 3,000 to that Shavuot moment when the Spirit descended.

Chapter 6: The Two Messiahs - Prophecy Fulfilled

Well, we're at a turning point in our detective story, and this one's going to light a fire under you. We've tracked the Zadok priesthood from the Sinai Covenant, through their exile after the

Maccabean revolt, and seen how their Essene followers, using the solar calendar, were the 3000 believers who responded to Peter's sermon in Acts 2. Their beliefs in the Holy Spirit and the pure Torah set them apart from the Pharisees and Sadducees. But now, we're diving into the biggest clue yet: the prophecy of **The Two Messiahs!** That's right—not one, but two anointed figures, a priestly Messiah and a kingly one, expected by the Essenes and rooted in ancient scriptures. This idea, found in Zechariah, Malachi, and the Dead Sea Scrolls, points straight to John the Baptist and Yeshua as the fulfillment. It's like finding the missing piece of a puzzle that makes the whole picture snap into focus. This is where the mystery of the 3000 starts to shine.

The Two Messiahs: A Prophecy Older Than Time

The idea of two Messiahs isn't something you hear in most churches, but it was a big deal for the Israelites. It seems like a secret to us but it was common knowledge during the first century. Under murderous Roman oppression – Israel was a powder keg – everyone awaiting anxiously the arrival of the two Messiahs. The Essenes, and many others, didn't just expect one savior; they looked for two anointed figures—one a priest, the other a king—to restore Israel. This belief comes from ancient prophecies, preserved in the Essenes' scrolls. The Essenes, following the Zadok tradition, expected two Messiahs based on scripture. One from the priestly line of Aaron, the other from the kingly line of David. This wasn't a wild guess; it was grounded in the Hebrew Bible and amplified in the Dead Sea Scrolls.

Let's start with Zechariah 4:11-14, which says, "These are the two anointed ones, that stand by the Lord of the whole earth." The Hebrew word for "anointed ones" is *meshiach*, meaning Messiah. Zechariah's vision shows two figures, symbolized as olive trees, anointed as "sons of fresh oil," standing beside God. One is a priest, the other a ruler. This dual role echoes the structure God set up at Sinai: a partnership between priests to

Chapter 6: The Two Messiahs Prophecy

advise and handle worship, kings to lead the nation. The Essenes recognized this as the prophecy of two Messiahs coming together to bring God's kingdom.

Then there's Malachi 3:1-2, in the oldest biblical text in existence, straight from the Dead Sea Scrolls 4Q76 Malachi says, "Behold, I will send my <u>messenger</u>, and he shall prepare the way before me: and the <u>Lord</u>, whom you seek, shall suddenly come to his temple". "And who can abide *them* when *they* come". That's plural—not one, but **two** figures. The Greeks did not want two Messiahs, they only wanted One Christ, so they basically tossed this prophecy. The Greek verse says "who can abide <u>him</u> when <u>he</u> comes" despite the fact the text is clearly referring to two figures. The Essenes had the original Hebrew text. Essenes read this as a priestly Messiah preparing the way and a kingly Messiah arriving to rule. This wasn't a new idea; it was rooted in their Zadokite heritage, which preserved the pure Torah and its prophecies.

The Dead Sea Scrolls: A Window into Zadokite Legacy

The Dead Sea Scrolls, preserved at Qumran by the Essenes, are a treasure chest of golden evidence! The Community Rule (1QS) and the Damascus Document talk about the "Sons of Zadok" awaiting a "Teacher of Righteousness" along with another Messiah— two Messiahs - one of the line of Aaron (priestly) and one of the line of David (kingly). The Essenes believed in a priestly Messiah to restore the true priesthood and a kingly Messiah to rule justly. They saw themselves as the remnant preparing for both. Their scrolls, like 1QSa, describe a future banquet where these two Messiahs lead together, one blessing the bread, the other the wine.

Yeshua: The Kingly Messiah

Enter Yeshua, the kingly Messiah. The Essenes expected a

descendant of David, and Yeshua's lineage checks out. In the Hebrew Text Version of Matthew 1:1-17, his genealogy traces through David, including *goels* like Tamar and Ruth—redeemers who kept the line holy. Matthew 1:1 declares, "The book of the generation of Yeshua the Messiah, the son of David" (HTV). This isn't just a family tree; it's a claim to the throne.

Yeshua's mission complemented John's. While John prepared the way with repentance, Yeshua brought the kingdom. In Matthew 4:17, he preaches, "Repent: for the kingdom of heaven is at hand". His miracles, teachings, and resurrection fulfilled the Essenes' belief was that of a kingly Messiah who'd restore God's rule. When Peter preached in Acts 2:22-24, saying, "Yeshua of Nazareth, a man approved of God among you by miracles and wonders and signs… ye have taken, and by wicked hands have crucified and slain: Whom God hath raised up", it was music to Essene ears. They believed in resurrection, unlike the Sadducees, and saw Yeshua as the Davidic king.

The Acts 2 Connection: Why the Essenes Were Ready

Here's the big clue tying this to our mystery: the Essenes' expectation of two Messiahs made them uniquely prepared for Acts 2. The Pharisees, along with most of the Israelites, wanted a Davidic warrior-king, not a suffering servant, like Joseph of the many-colored coat, along with a priestly forerunner. The Sadducees rejected the whole idea. But the Essenes, with their Zadokite roots, were waiting for both John and Yeshua. When Peter quoted Joel—"I will pour out of my Spirit upon all flesh" (Acts 2:17)—and tied it to Yeshua's resurrection, the Essenes in the crowd saw their prophecies coming true. The 3000 baptized were a response to a dual Messiahship they'd been expecting for generations.

Essenes went through a 3-year apprenticeship seeking the truth of Scripture led by the Holy Spirit (the *Community Rule*). When they were ready, they were initiated into the Essene community on Shavuot

Chapter 6: The Two Messiahs Prophecy

at the Temple in Jerusalem. They were there expecting to be baptized by the Holy Spirit.

The 3000 were Essenes—their beliefs aligned with Peter's message—two Messiahs, the Holy Spirit, and a dedication to the New Covenant.

Their Zadok calendar put them in Jerusalem on the right day of Shavuot. Their faith in a priestly and kingly Messiah sealed the deal.

A Dark Footnote: The Cover-Up Continues

One chilling detail: the Hasmoneans tried to erase the prophecy with the burning of the Zadokite records. Later Herod tried to erase the prophets, John and Yeshua. The *Protoevangelium of James* claims Zachariah, John's father, was murdered in the Temple because he refused to give up the whereabouts of his son John whom Herod wished to kill. Herod hunted both John and Yeshua, fearing their Messianic roles.

The Next Clue: John's Zadokite Roots

This two-Messiah prophecy is a cornerstone, but it raises a question: how deep were John the Baptist's ties to the Essenes and Zadokites? Was he raised among them, trained in their ways? Do we really have any evidence of this as we have claimed? That's our next lead, and it's going to take us deeper into the wilderness where the Essenes kept the flame alive. What if John's life experience holds the key to why the 3000 were so ready?

Chapter 7: John the Baptist - The Priestly Messiah

We're peeling back another layer of this mystery, and this one's a doozy. We've followed the Zadok priesthood from the covenant at Sinai, through their exile after the Maccabean revolt, to the Essenes who carried their torch, using the solar calendar and expecting two Messiahs. Last chapter, we saw how those prophecies pointed to John the Baptist as the priestly Messiah and Yeshua as the kingly one, perfectly aligning with Scripture and the Essenes' beliefs - explaining why the 3,000 believers in Acts 2 were "sons of Zadok." Now, we're zooming in on John the Baptist himself—his Zadokite roots, his wilderness upbringing, and his role as the priestly Messiah who prepared the way for Yeshua. This isn't just a side story; it's the spark that lit the fire for those 3,000. We're about to uncover how John's life ties directly to our mystery. Buckle up—this is where the trail gets personal.

Now, let's meet the first figure: John the Baptist. The Essenes' priestly Messiah had to come from Aaron's line, and John fits the bill perfectly. Luke 1:5 tells us, "There was in the days of Herod, the king of Judaea, a certain priest named Zachariah, of the course of Abia: and his wife was of the daughters of Aaron, and her name was Elisabeth." The priestly course of Abia was composed of the "Sons of Zadok" (1 Chronicles 24:3-19).

Chapter 7: John the Baptist's Zadokite Roots

Zachariah, John's father, was a righteous priest serving in the Temple. His wife, Elisabeth, was also from Aaron's line, putting John squarely in the direct line of the Zadok priesthood. John, like his father Zachariah, was a priest, "a son of Zadok!"

But John wasn't your typical Temple priest. He grew up in the wilderness, among the Essenes at Qumran. Luke 1:80 says, "And the child grew, and waxed strong in spirit, and was in the deserts till the day of his shewing unto Israel". Why the wilderness? Because the Essenes, exiled after the Maccabean revolt, lived in the wilderness of Qumran, as it was called, rejecting the corruption of the Jerusalem priests. John's fiery preaching—calling the Pharisees and Sadducees "vipers" in Matthew 3:7—echoes the Essenes' War Scroll, pitting the "Sons of Light" against the "Sons of Darkness" (1QM).

John's role as the priestly Messiah in Malachi 3:1 is clear, he is the "messenger" preparing the way. The angel Gabriel told Zachariah, "He shall be filled with the Holy Ghost, even from his mother's womb. And many of the children of Israel shall he turn to the Lord their God" (Luke 1:15-16). John's baptism of repentance was about cleansing Israel, a priestly act, setting the stage for the kingly Messiah. The Essenes, expecting this, would've seen John as the priestly Messiah, fulfilling their scrolls. John was, after all, one of them raised from a child in Qumran. As it was prophesized, John turned many, especially among the Essenes, toward the coming of the Teacher of Righteousness, Yeshua Ha Mashiach. The Essenes believed that the Teacher had come and that he would return.

John's Lineage: Born to the Priesthood

Luke 1:5 sets the stage: "There was in the days of Herod, the king of Judaea, a certain priest named Zachariah, of the course of Abijah: and his wife was of the daughters of Aaron, and her name was Elisabeth." Zachariah, John's father, was a priest from the division of Abijah, one of the 24 priestly courses set up by Zadok for King

David (1 Chronicles 24:10). That's how we know that those in the course of Abijah were composed of the "sons of Zadok!" It is right there in Chronicles as clear as day. Elisabeth, his mother, was also from Aaron's line, making John a pure descendant of the original priestly line Yehovah established at Sinai.

This wasn't just a random priestly gig; it was a direct link to the Zadokites, the righteous priests who served faithfully under David and Solomon. The "sons of Zadok" were those whom Yehovah granted the priesthood of the eternal Temple in heaven for all time (Exekiel 40:46). They were the only priests allowed in the direct presence of Yehovah in order to serve him. Those are the highest honors conceivable for a priest and a priesthood and should not be ignored or diminished by anyone who believes in the truth of Scripture.

The fact is that the descendants of the Hasmoneans (the Maccabees) had deposed His godly priesthood and the Jewish people never restored it! They never went back to what Yehovah had ordained. Think about that. So the question is, was Yehovah seeking to re-establish the godly line of priests and their followers through John and Yeshua? Deserves some thought – does it not?

The Wilderness Connection: Raised Among the Essenes

John didn't grow up in the Temple, though. Luke 1:80 tells us, "And the child grew, and waxed strong in spirit, and was in the deserts till the day of his shewing unto Israel." Why the desert? Because that's where the Essenes lived after the Maccabean revolt kicked the Zadokites out of Jerusalem. Places like Qumran, near the Dead Sea, were their strongholds, where they preserved the solar calendar, the pure Torah, and prophecies about the Messiahs. Qumran was a hub for the "Sons of Zadok," who were the remnant of God's true priesthood.

John was raised among the Essenes at Qumran. His parents

were old when he was born, so they would have entrusted him to their own Zadokite community to protect him from Herod's murderous intentions! Herod, who had an extensive secret police, immediately assassinated anyone who had a claim to the throne (Yeshua) or the high priesthood (John). The apocryphal *Protoevangelium of James* says Zachariah was murdered by Herod's secret police in the Temple for not giving up his son John to be slain, a story that illustrates quite clearly the suppression Zadokites lived under. Sending John to the wilderness insured his survival and steeped him in Essene teachings.

The Essenes' scrolls, like the *Community Rule* (1QS), describe a rigorous upbringing for their members—study, purity, and preparation for the Messiahs. John's ascetic lifestyle—no fancy clothes, eating locusts and honey (Matthew 3:4, HTV)—matches the Essenes, who ate locusts and were famous for their date honey.

This was a coded message in Scripture. We often typify groups of people by the foods they eat. If in old WWII movies, one said someone was a "kraut" you would know them to be German because they eat sourkraut. If one said someone was a "limey" you would know them to be English, whose historic sailors ate limes to protect against scurvy. If one said someone was a "frog" you could think he was French because they eat frogs. To the people of the first century in Israel, everyone would know the "locust and honey" reference meant John was an Essene. His wilderness preaching, calling for repentance and baptism, was straight out of the Essene playbook, echoing their belief in the Holy Spirit and the New Covenant!

John as the Priestly Messiah: Preparing the Way

The Essenes expected a priestly Messiah from Aaron's line to purify Israel's worship, based on prophecies like Malachi 3:1: "Behold, I will send my messenger, and he shall prepare the way before me." John was that messenger, the priestly figure paving the way for Yeshua. Luke 1:17 says the angel Gabriel told Zachariah that John would go "in the spirit and power of Elijah, to turn the hearts of the fathers to the children, and the disobedient to the wisdom of the just; to make ready a people prepared for the Lord."

John's mission was priestly to the core. His baptism wasn't just a dunk in the Jordan; it was a cleansing ritual, like the Zadokites' purification rites described in Ezekiel 44:23: "And they shall teach my people the difference between the holy and profane, and cause them to discern between the unclean and the clean." He called out the corrupt leaders—Pharisees and Sadducees—as "vipers" in Matthew 3:7: "O generation of vipers, who hath warned you to flee from the wrath to come?" This echoes the Essenes' War Scroll (1QM), which pits the "Sons of Light" against the "Sons of Darkness"—the false priests and their allies.

John was the priestly Messiah, preparing Israel by calling them back to the pure covenant of Moses - while ushering them forward to the New Covenant of Yeshua. His baptism was about repentance, a Zadokite act to restore holiness. The Essenes, waiting for this figure, would've recognized John immediately. His message aligned with their scrolls, like the *Damascus Document*, which calls for a return to the Torah and entering into the New Covenant.

The Acts 2 Connection: John's Role in Priming the 3000

Here's where John ties directly to our mystery. The 3000 believers in Acts 2 weren't starting from scratch; they were primed by John's ministry. Many of the Es-senes had heard John preach or been baptized by him. Especially those at Qumran, but remember the Zadokites were dispersed all over the map. There was an Essene quarter in Jerusalem, Essenes in every village of Judea, the headquarters of the Essene movement in Damascus, a massive Temple in Leontopolis in Egypt, and evidence of them in Arabia, Syria, Jordon and further afield.

They were all over the region – a movement - far, far more than a few hermits by the Dead Sea. Mark 1:5 says, "And there went out unto him (John) all the land of Judea, and they of Jerusalem, and were all baptized of him in the river of Jordan, confessing their sins." At Shavuot the "righteous" *(tzadekim=Zadokites)* of all the nations were come to Jerusalem. Those Essene Zadokites living near the Jordan in Qumran, were already John's followers, ready for the next step—Yeshua's arrival.

When Peter preached at Shavuot, he built on John's foundation. Acts 2:38 says, "Repent, and be baptized every one of you in the name of Jesus Christ for the remission of sins, and you shall receive the gift of the Holy Spirit." That's John's message—repentance and baptism—plus the Spirit's outpouring, which the Essenes expected (1QS). The 3,000 responded because John had already prepared their hearts, fulfilling his role as the priestly Messiah. John's work set the stage for Acts 2. The Essenes were ready because he was their Teacher of Righteousness.

The Threat to Herod: The True High Priest Zachariah

Zachariah's Zadokite roots made him a threat, a claimant to the high priesthood. In Luke 1:11 the Archangel Gabriel appears to Zachariah and appoints him to a mission, that of having a son (John), conceiving, caring, preparing and passing that anointment of the Holy Spirit to him (Luke 1:15). For those who don't understand what just happened here, when Yehovah sends his archangel Gabriel into the Temple to anoint a particular priest – that priest is now the high priest of Israel – unless, of course, you can find another priest with better credentials than being anointed by God Almighty.

The text of *The Protoevangelium of James*, written by Yeshua's brother, tells the story of Zachariah's murder by Herod Antipas in chapter 23, verse 9. This was also revealed in the Gospel of Luke 11:51, "Zachariah, whom you murdered between the sanctuary and the altar!" The Herodian line of kings would have assassinated any one with such a claim to power immediately. Since the high priesthood was, to some degree, hereditary – that anointment of Gabriel to Zachariah was passed to John the Baptist making him then the true high priest of Israel - the only person capable of baptizing the king!

Matthew 14:3-10 tells how Herod later beheaded John. And let us not forget the slaughter of the children of Bethlehem by Herod Magnus in order to kill the infant Messiah prophesied by the three Wise Men from Babylon to be the coming king of Israel. This bloodlust for power was the same motivation that caused the burning of Zadokite records, trying to erase the true priesthood. The coming king and the true high priest of Israel. Both were targeted. Both were martyred.

The Essenes - still oppressed and keeping their heads down in the wilderness of Qumran - represented John's legacy. Their scrolls and Zadok priests kept the faith alive, leading to the moment in Acts 2 when their followers—the first 3000—stepped into history!

The Next Clue: Yeshua's Role

John prepared the way, but Yeshua was the kingly Messiah, the other half of the prophecy. How did his Davidic lineage and mission complement John's? And how did the Essenes recognize him? That's our next lead, and it's going to show why the 3000 saw Yeshua as the fulfillment of their prophecies. The Essenes were renowned for their prophetic ability in the first century.

Chapter 8: Yeshua - The Kingly Messiah

We're closing in on the heart of this mystery, and this chapter's going to hit like a thunderbolt. We've traced the Zadokite priesthood from Sinai, through their exile, to the Essenes who carried their torch, following the Zadok calendar and expecting two Messiahs. Last chapter, we saw John the Baptist as the priestly Messiah, preparing the way with his wilderness preaching and Zadokite roots. Now, we turn to Yeshua, the kingly Messiah, whose lineage and mission fulfilled the other half of the Essene prophecy. Those 3000 believers in Acts 2 weren't just moved by Peter's preaching - they saw Yeshua as the *Teacher of Righteousness* they'd been waiting for, rooted in prophecies they cherished. We'll uncover how Yeshua's royal bloodline and actions matched the Essenes' hopes. This is the second piece of the Messianic puzzle, and it's going to show why those 3000 were ready to follow him. Let's dive in!

Yeshua's Lineage: The Son of David

To understand Yeshua as the kingly Messiah, we start with his roots, and they're as royal as it gets. The Essenes, steeped in Zadokite tradition, expected a Messiah from David's line, based on prophecies like 2 Samuel 7:12-13, where God tells David, "I will set up thy seed after thee... and I will stablish his kingdom. He shall build an house for my name, and I will stablish the throne of his kingdom forever." This wasn't just any king; it was a promised ruler to restore Israel.

The Hebrew Text Version of Matthew lays it out clear as day. Matthew 1:1 declares, "The book of the generation of Yeshua the Messiah, the son of David, the son of Abraham" (HTV). This isn't just a fancy title; it's a claim to the throne. The genealogy in Matthew 1:2-17 traces Yeshua's line through David, hitting key figures like Judah, Hezekiah, and Zerubbabel (HTV). Why does this matter? The Essenes were looking for a kingly Messiah from David's line, and Yeshua's genealogy in Matthew was proof he fit the bill. It's like a legal document for royalty.

His genealogy is a legal document of descent from royalty!

Not to mention that seven generations back, on his father Joseph's side, one of Yeshua's ancestors was Zadok! (Matthew 1:14) This would not have been the high priest Zadok but one of his descendants, since they take the names of their ancestors. So it seems that Yeshua, although of the royal line, still had a Zadokite connection. This is typically missed in translation. In Hebrew the name is pronounced either as "Tzadok" or "Tsadok", a beginning sound English-speakers are not used to - so the T is usually dropped. In the KJV it is written "Sadoc" from "Tsadok" but in the Hebrew text of Matthew it is "Tzadok."

The Kingly Messiah: Yeshua's Mission

The Essenes didn't just want a king with the right bloodline; they expected a Messiah who'd restore God's kingdom, defeat evil, and rule justly. Their Dead Sea Scrolls, like 1QSa, describe a kingly Messiah leading alongside a priestly one, as we saw with John the Baptist. Zechariah 4:14 "two anointed ones" pointed to this duo, and the scroll 4Q76 Malachi 3:1-2 declares "them," confirming two Messiahs. Yeshua was the true king of Israel.

Matthew 4:17 captures Yeshua's mission: "From that time Yeshua began to preach, and to say, Repent: for the kingdom of heaven is at hand." This wasn't just talk; it was a royal decree. The Essenes, per their scrolls, expected a king to bring God's rule, and Yeshua's preaching about the kingdom hit that note. His miracles—healing the sick, casting out demons, raising the dead—showed divine authority. Yeshua fought his battles with supernatural weapons, not earthly ones. Peter's sermon in Acts 2:22 sums it up: "Yeshua of Nazareth, a man approved of God among you by miracles and wonders and signs, which God did by him in the midst of you." For the Essenes, who believed in resurrection unlike the Sadducees, Yeshua's signs were proof he was the real deal.

Yeshua's teaching also aligned with Essene values. In Matthew 5:17-18, he says, "Do not think - I came that I might breach (break) the Torah - or the prophets. I came not that I might fulfill (complete or end) but rather that I might fill (the Torah) to overflowing, abundantly overflowing!" (HTV). This matched the Essenes' commitment to the pure written Torah, without the Pharisees' extra rules. Yeshua's focus on the Torah's spirit, not man-made traditions, was exactly what the Essenes taught.

The Resurrection: The King's Victory

The Essenes' belief in resurrection was a big deal, and Yeshua's rising from the dead sealed his role as kingly Messiah. The Sadducees scoffed at resurrection, and the Pharisees debated it, but the Essenes' scrolls, like 4Q521, describe a Messiah who'd raise the dead and heal the broken. When Peter preached in Acts 2:24, "Whom God hath raised up, having loosed the pains of death: because it was not possible that he should be holden of it", it was a direct hit for the Essenes. They saw Yeshua's resurrection as the ultimate sign of his Messianic kingship.

This ties straight to our mystery. The 3000 believers in Acts 2 responded because they recognized Yeshua as the Davidic king they'd been waiting for, fulfilling their scrolls' prophecies. Their communal living—sharing all things (Acts 2:44-45)—mirrored the Essenes' lifestyle, showing they were already living out the kingdom Yeshua preached.

Yeshua and John: The Perfect Pair

The Essenes' two-Messiah prophecy meant John and Yeshua were a team. John, the priestly Messiah, prepared Israel through repentance and baptism, cleansing the people. Yeshua, the kingly Messiah, brought the kingdom, teaching and proving it through miracles and resurrection. Matthew 11:11-13 shows Yeshua honoring John: "Among them that are born of women, there hath not risen a greater than John the Baptist... For all the prophets and the Torah prophesied until John" (HTV). John paved the way; Yeshua fulfilled it.

The Essenes saw John and Yeshua as the two anointed ones. John's priestly role set the stage, and Yeshua's kingly role brought the kingdom. That's why the 3,000 were ready. The Essenes, on their solar calendar, were in Jerusalem for Shavuot, primed by John's preaching and ready for Yeshua's victory.

The Threat to Power: Herod's Fear

Yeshua's royal claim wasn't just spiritual; it was a threat to the status quo. Herod the Great, who hunted John's family, also sought to kill Yeshua as a baby (Matthew 2:16). Why? Because a true Davidic king challenged his puppet rule and the corrupt Hasmonean priesthood. The burning of Zadokite records, as we saw in Chapter 3, aimed to erase prophecies like the two Messiahs, keeping power in the wrong hands. Yeshua's lineage and mission were a direct challenge to that cover-up.

The Acts 2 Connection: Why the First 3000 Believed

The 3000 in Acts 2 were likely Essenes because Yeshua's life matched their kingly Messiah prophecy. Peter's sermon, quoting Psalm 16 about the resurrection—"Thou wilt not leave my soul in hell, neither wilt thou suffer thine Holy One to see corruption" (Acts 2:27, KJV)—resonated with their scrolls. Their Zadokite roots, John's preparation, and Yeshua's fulfillment made them leap at the chance to join "the Way" (Acts 9:2, KJV).

But there's another layer to explore. If the Essenes were the 3,000, what was life like in their Qumran community? How did their practices shape the early believers? That's our next clue, and it's going to take us deep into the desert to uncover their secrets.

Chapter 9: The Essenes' Qumran Community - Secrets of the Scrolls

Now, we're getting closer to cracking this mystery wide open, and this chapter's like stumbling into a hidden vault full of ancient treasures. We've followed the Zadokite priesthood from Sinai, through their exile after the Maccabean revolt, to their Essene followers who used a solar calendar and expected two Messiahs—John the Baptist as the priestly one and Yeshua as the kingly. Those 3,000 believers in Acts 2, we've argued, were likely Essenes, primed by their beliefs and John's preaching to receive Peter's message. Now, we're heading into the heart of Essene life: their community at Qumran, near the Dead Sea, where they preserved their faith in exile. The Dead Sea Scrolls, found in caves there, are like a time capsule, revealing their practices, beliefs, and why they were ready for the Messiah. We'll uncover how the Qumran community shaped the 3,000. This is where the trail gets vivid—let's step into the desert and see what secrets the scrolls hold.

Qumran: A Fortress of Faith

Picture a rugged, sun-scorched landscape by the Dead Sea, about 20 miles east of Jerusalem. That's where Qumran sits, a cluster of buildings and caves where the Essenes lived in the centuries before and during Yeshua's time. After the Maccabean revolt ousted the Zadokites around 152 BC, many fled here, forming a monastic community dedicated to preserving God's covenant. Qumran was like a spiritual fortress for the Essenes. They saw themselves as the true Israel, keeping the Zadokite faith alive in the wilderness.

Archaeologists found evidence of this at Qumran: communal dining halls, ritual baths (*mikvahs*), and a scriptorium where they copied scrolls. This wasn't a vacation spot; it was a place of discipline, study, and worship. The Essenes lived simply, sharing everything, much like the believers in Acts 2:44-45: "And all that believed were together, and had all things common; and sold their possessions and goods, and parted them to all men, as every man had need." That's no coincidence—it's a clue that the 3,000 were Essenes, living out Qumran's communal ideals.

The Dead Sea Scrolls: A Window into Essene Life

The real treasure at Qumran is the Dead Sea Scrolls, discovered in 1947 in nearby caves. These manuscripts—over 900 of them—

are a library of Essene thought, written between 200 BC and 70 AD. They include copies of the Hebrew Bible, commentaries, and community rules. The scrolls show us the Essenes' heart—their commitment to the pure Torah, the Holy Spirit, and the coming Messiahs. Let's unpack a few key scrolls to see how they connect to our mystery.

First, the *Community Rule*. This scroll lays out the Essenes' way of life: strict obedience to the Torah, communal living, and guidance by the Holy Spirit. It calls them "Sons of Zadok," tying them directly to the righteous priesthood we've been tracking.

They saw themselves as a remnant, preparing for God's kingdom.

The scroll says members must "separate from the congregation of the men of injustice" (1QS, 5:1-2), meaning the corrupt Temple priests and Pharisees. Sound familiar? That's the same spirit as John the Baptist's preaching against the "vipers" (Matthew 3:7).

Second, the *Damascus Document*. This text describes the Essenes' exile to "Damascus" after the Zadokite expulsion. It says, "The priests, the Levites, and the sons of Zadok who kept the charge of the sanctuary when the children of Israel went astray" (CD, 3:21-4:2). They were preserving the true covenant, waiting for a "Teacher of Righteousness" to guide them. Many scholars think John the Baptist trained by the Essenes. John was not simply linked to Qumran - he lived there! He baptized Israelites in the Jordan only a short walk from Qumran.

Third, the *War Scroll*. This one's intense—it describes an end-time battle between the "Sons of Light" (the Essenes) and the "Sons of Darkness" (corrupt priests and their allies). It's full of hope for a divine victory led by the two Messiahs. This matches John's fiery call to repentance and Yeshua's preaching "the kingdom is near!"

Peter echoed this in Acts 2:38: "Repent, and be baptized every one of you in the name of Jesus Christ for the remission of sins, and you shall receive the gift of the Holy Spirit."

Beliefs That Primed the 3,000

The scrolls reveal why the Essenes were ready for Acts 2. First, their belief in the Holy Spirit. The *Community Rule* says God's Spirit would cleanse the faithful and guide them to truth (1QS, 4:6). When Peter quoted Joel—"I will pour out of my Spirit upon all flesh" (Acts 2:17)—it was like a signal flare for the Essenes. They were expecting this outpouring, unlike the Pharisees, who leaned on rules, or the Sadducees, who denied the Spirit.

Second, their hope for two Messiahs. The scrolls, like 1QSa, describe a priestly Messiah (John) and a kingly one (Yeshua), as we saw in Chapter 6. Zechariah 4:14's "two anointed ones" and 4Q76's plural "them" in Malachi 3:1-2 fueled this hope. The 3,000, likely Essenes, saw John's baptism and Yeshua's resurrection as the fulfillment, making Peter's testimony a call they couldn't ignore.

Third, the New Covenant. The Essenes' belief in the New Covenant (Jeremiah 31:31) was stated as a central tenet of their faith as expressed in The Damascus Document (originally known as The Zadok Document). The first line of that document says, "For those entering into the New Covenant in the land of Damascus." Seems pretty clear, the Essene/Zadokites were all about the New Covenant and everything that goes with it.

The Zadok Calendar: Right Place, Right Time

The scrolls also confirm the Essenes' use of the 364-day solar calendar, as we discussed in Chapter 5. The *Calendrical Texts* (4Q320-321) detail how they fixed feast days like Shavuot, unlike the Pharisees' shifting lunar calendar. This is huge for our mystery. Acts 2:1 says the Spirit fell "when the day of Pentecost was fully come." The Essenes' Shavuot, on their Zadok calendar, differed from the Pharisees' date based on the observation of the barley harvest to fix the day of Passover, then 49 more days until Shavuot. The Sadducees counted the Omer differently, the days and Sabbaths between Passover and Shavuot. So, their Shavuot was not on the same day either. The 3000 were there because they followed the Zadokite calendar, putting them in

John's Qumran Connection

John the Baptist's wilderness upbringing was at Qumran. His family were Zadokites. They had ties there. We know that Qumran did take in children/acolytes to be raised in the faith. Elizabeth took John there even before Herod's secret police thugs came looking for John, and not finding his whereabouts, they slaughtered Zachariah between the sanctuary (the Holy of Holies) and the altar. Both Zachariah and Elizabeth were warned by the angel. As for John, Luke 1:80 says he "was in the wilderness till the day of his shewing unto Israel." The Essenes' ritual baths at Qumran align with John's baptism in the Jordan, a cleansing rite for repentance (Matthew 3:6, HTV). The *Damascus Document* calls for such purifications, and John's call to "bring forth fruits meet for repentance" (Matthew 3:8) echoes the Essenes' focus on holiness. He was raised on their teachings, and that of the Spirit preparing the 3000 for Yeshua.

The Cover-Up's Shadow

The scrolls also hint at the ongoing cover-up we uncovered. The Essenes hid their manuscripts in caves to protect them from destruction. Who would want to destroy their records? The same kind of people who did it the first time. Then it was the Hasmonean kings backed by the Greeks. By Yeshua's time it was the Herodian kings backed by the Romans. The Zadokites had been targeted, their high priest Onias III assassinated. Other priests and followers were expelled from Jerusalem. They had lived under oppression for so long, keeping their heads down, it was habitual.

There was a delicate balance between the powers-that-be in Jerusalem and the Essenes. As long as the Zadokites didn't meddle with the status quo they were tolerated. However, they knew if they attempted to take back their birthright of the Temple it would mean their destruction.

The burning of Zadokite records left gaps in history, the Qumran scrolls were either surviving scrolls from the Temple, or a reconstruction of the Zadok scrolls that had been destroyed, or both, plus some of their own writings. They ripped up their own scrolls when surrounded by the Romans in their last days. Their secrecy about the scrolls was the primary indication of just how dangerous their beliefs were to the powers-that-be in Jerusalem.

The Acts 2 Connection: Qumran's Legacy

The Qumran community shaped the 3,000 believers. Their scrolls' emphasis on the Spirit, two Messiahs, and communal living matched the events of Acts 2. When Peter preached about Yeshua's resurrection and the Spirit's outpouring, the Essenes saw their prophecies fulfilled. Their solar calendar put them in Jerusalem at the right moment, and their Zadokite roots, through John, prepared their hearts. Qumran was the training ground for the 3,000. They were the remnant, ready for the Messiah.

But what about their exile to "Damascus"? The *Damascus Document* states that a central Zadokite headquarters there. Could this be another key to the 3000's identity? That's our next clue, and it's going to take us beyond Qumran to uncover their final stand.

Chapter 10: The Damascus Document - Zadokite Exile Unveiled

We're hot on the trail of this mystery, and this chapter's like finding a hidden map in an old chest. We've followed the Zadokite priesthood from their roots at Sinai, through their exile after the Maccabean revolt, to the Essenes at Qumran, where their scrolls revealed their faith in two Messiahs—John the Baptist and Yeshua—priming the 3000 believers for Acts 2. Now, we're zeroing in on a key piece of evidence: the *Damascus Document*, a Dead Sea Scroll that tells of the Zadokites' exile to "Damascus" after their ousting from Jerusalem. This isn't just a dusty manuscript; it's a window into how the Essenes preserved their faith during the diaspora, keeping the flame of the true covenant alive. We'll uncover how this exile shaped the 3000 believers. Get ready—this trail's taking us from Qumran to ancient "Damascus," and it's going to tie our mystery together in ways you won't believe.

The Damascus Document: A Scroll of Exile

The *Damascus Document*, is one of the most revealing texts

found among the Dead Sea Scrolls at Qumran. Written between the 2nd century BC and 1st century AD, it's like a manifesto for the Essenes, detailing their history, beliefs, and rules. It was a roadmap of the Zadokite remnant's journey after they were kicked out of the Temple. It's not just a rulebook; it's a story of survival, faith, and hope for restoration.

The document starts with a history lesson, describing how God punished Israel for straying but preserved a remnant: "The priests, the Levites, and the sons of Zadok who kept the charge of the sanctuary when the children of Israel went astray" (CD, 3:21-4:2). This points straight to the Maccabean revolt around 152 BC, when the Hasmoneans ousted the Zadokites, as we saw in Chapter 3. The "sons of Zadok" fled to "Damascus," where they formed a new covenant community. The text says, "Those who held fast escaped to the land of the north, and He raised up for them a Teacher of Righteousness to guide them in the way of His heart" (CD, 1:11-12).

Damascus: The New Headquarters of the Zadokite Movement

The *Damascus Document* spells out how the Essenes lived in exile. They followed the 364-day solar calendar, as we saw in Chapter 5, ensuring feasts like Shavuot were on God's timing. They rejected the Hasmonean Temple's lunar calendar and corrupt priests, whom they called the "congregation of traitors" (CD, 1:12). Their rules were strict: no stealing, no impure acts, and a commitment to communal sharing, much like Acts 2:44-45: "And all that believed were together, and had all things common."

The Damascus community was about preserving the Zadokite priesthood's purity—Torah, calendar, and hope for the New Covenant. That's why they were ready for Acts 2. Their belief in the Holy Spirit, seen in scrolls like 1QS, matched Peter's preaching about the Spirit's outpouring (Acts 2:17). Their expectation of a priestly and kingly Messiah, as in Zechariah 4:14's "two anointed ones", made them see John and Yeshua as the fulfillment.

The Acts 2 Connection: The Exiles' Return

Here's the big clue for our mystery: the *Damascus Document* shows why the 3,000 were in Jerusalem at Shavuot. The Essenes, whether in Qumran or a broader "Damascus" network, made pilgrimages to Jerusalem for feasts on their solar calendar. Acts 2:5 says, "And there were dwelling at Jerusalem Jews, devout men, out of every nation under heaven.". These "devout men" were Essenes, including those from "Damascus," gathered for Shavuot on the Zadok solar calendar, not the Pharisees' lunar one. When Peter preached about Yeshua's resurrection and the Spirit, it hit their prophetic expectations dead-on.

The *Damascus Document's* focus on a "New Covenant" also echoes Acts 2. The Essenes saw themselves as renewing the covenant God gave at Sinai, which the Hasmoneans corrupted. Peter's call to "repent, and be baptized" was a call to join this renewed covenant, which the 3000—steeped in Essene teachings— embraced. The 3000 were Essenes drawn from communities throughout the region, responding to the Messiah they'd been waiting for. Although there were some differences in these far-flung diaspora communities of Zadokites, their basic beliefs were the same.

The Next Clue: Paul's Role

The *Damascus Document* ties the Essenes to "the Way," a term used in Acts 9:2 for early believers. This leads us to Paul, who persecuted "the Way" in Damascus before his conversion. Was he chasing Essenes? And how did their teachings shape him? That's our next lead, and it's going to shake up our understanding of the early believers.

Chapter 11: Paul and the Way - From Persecutor to Disciple

This chapter's like finding a hidden letter that changes everything. We've traced the Zadokite priesthood from Sinai, through their exile after the Maccabean revolt, to the Essenes who preserved their faith in Qumran and "Damascus," expecting two Messiahs—John the Baptist and Yeshua. Those 3000 believers in Acts 2, were Essenes, primed by their solar calendar and beliefs to receive Peter's sermon. Now, we turn to a surprising figure: Paul, the man who started as a fierce persecutor of "the Way" but became its greatest advocate. His story, especially his connection to Damascus and the Essenes, is a crucial clue in understanding the 3,000 and the early Messianic movement. We'll uncover how Paul's persecution, conversion, and learning from the Essenes shaped the faith that spread from Acts 2. Get ready—this trail's about to take a wild turn!

Paul's Persecution: Targeting "the Way"

Before he was Paul, he was Saul, a Pharisee with a mission to crush the early believers. Acts 9:1-2 sets the scene: "And Saul, yet breathing out threatenings and slaughter against the disciples of the Lord, went unto the high priest, and desired of him letters to Damascus to the synagogues, that if he found any of *this way*, whether they were men or women, he might bring them bound unto Jerusalem." Notice that phrase—"the Way." It's not just a catchy name; it's a direct link to the Essenes. The *Damascus Document* and *Community Rule* (1QS) use "the Way" to describe their community, echoing Isaiah 35:8: "And an highway shall be there, and a way, and it shall be called The way of holiness." The Way in Acts is the same term the Essenes used. Paul was hunting Essenes or their followers in Damascus.

Why Damascus? As we saw in Chapter 10, "Damascus" in the *Damascus Document* was the literal headquarters of Essene communities in the region, where Zadokite exiles kept their faith alive (CD, 6:19). Paul, trained as a Pharisee under Gamaliel (Acts 22:3), saw these believers as a threat to Judaism, with its lunar calendar and Oral Torah. Their Zadokite roots, solar calendar, and belief in two Messiahs—John and Yeshua—challenged everything he stood for.

Paul targeted 'the Way' because their pure Torah and Messianic faith were a direct rebuke to the Pharisees' traditions.

Saul's most cherished hatred was toward Yeshua the Messiah, the son of God. What an abomination to Saul this was, a divine son to God, that is polytheism which cannot be allowed to live alongside of the One True God – not two – One God. Yeshua's movement was winding like a snake throughout the Essene communities of the region. The head of that snake was in Damascus!

Paul's persecution wasn't random, cut off the head of the snake and the Yeshua movement would be dead. Acts 8:3 says he "made havock of the church, entering into every house, and haling men and women committed them to prison." These early believers, Essenes or their converts, were the same folks as the 3000 in Acts 2, sharing all things in common (Acts 2:44-45). Paul's mission was to stamp out this Messianic movement before it spread.

The Road to Damascus: A Divine U-Turn

Then comes the plot twist. On his way to Damascus, Paul has a life-changing encounter. Acts 9:3-5 describes it: "And as he journeyed, he came near Damascus: and suddenly there shined round about him a light from heaven: And he fell to the earth, and heard a voice saying unto him, Saul, Saul, why persecutest thou me? And he said, Who art thou, Lord? And the Lord said, I am Jesus whom thou persecutest."

Yeshua himself stops Paul in his tracks, blinding him and redirecting his life.

This wasn't just a random spot on the map. Damascus was a center for "the Way," as the *Damascus Document* suggests (CD, 1:11). Paul was targeting Essene believers who followed John's baptism and Yeshua's teachings. After his encounter, Paul is led to Damascus, where Ananias, a disciple, restores his sight and baptizes him (Acts 9:17-18). Ananias was probably part of the Damascus community, an Essene himself, who helped Paul understand the Messianic faith. cripture says that Paul stayed there for three years among those he had been sent to "bring back in chains." Three years was the length of of the Essene apprenticeship before entering the movement.

Learning from the Essenes: Paul's Transformation

After his conversion, Paul didn't just flip a switch and start preaching. He needed to unlearn his Pharisaic traditions and embrace the pure Torah of "the Way." Galatians 1:17-18 says, "Neither went I up to Jerusalem to them which were apostles before me; but I went into Arabia, and returned again unto Damascus. Then after three years I went up to Jerusalem." Where did Paul go in Arabia? Some scholars suggest he went to

Mount Sinai in Arabia. After all, Paul is the one who identifies its location.

Paul spent 3 years with Essenes in Damascus, studying the Torah and scrolls that shaped "the Way".

The Essenes' teachings—rooted in the Zadokite priesthood—would've reshaped Paul's thinking. Their *Community Rule* emphasizes the Holy Spirit guiding the faithful, which aligns with Paul's later writings, like Romans 8:14: "For as many as are led by the Spirit of God, they are the sons of God." Their belief in two Messiahs, seen in Zechariah 4:14's "two anointed ones" and the *Damascus Document* (CD, 7:20-21), helped Paul see Yeshua as the kingly Messiah, complementing John's priestly role. The Hebrew Text Version of Matthew, which Paul may have encountered, reinforced this with Yeshua's words: "I came not that I might fulfill (complete or end) but rather that I might fill (the Torah) to overflowing" (Matthew 5:17, HTV).

Paul's time in Damascus likely exposed him to the solar calendar, too. The Essenes' 364-day calendar kept God's feasts pure, unlike the Pharisees' lunar one. This may have influenced Paul's focus on God's timing in his letters, like 1Corinthians 5:7-8, where he ties Passover to Yeshua's sacrifice.

The Acts 2 Connection: Paul and the 3000

How does this tie to our mystery? The 3000 believers in Acts 2 were Essenes, part of "the Way," as we've seen. Paul's persecution targeted their communities, but his conversion made him their champion. When he preached about Yeshua's resurrection and the Spirit, as Peter did in Acts 2:32-33, he was building on the same Essene beliefs—resurrection, the Spirit, and the Torah's purity—that drew the 3,000. His time with Essene believers in Damascus gave him the tools to spread their faith to the Gentiles, making "the Way" a global movement.

Paul went from destroying the Essenes to learning from them. Their teachings shaped his message, connecting the 3000 to the churches he founded. The communal living of Acts 2:44-45, rooted in Essene practices, became a hallmark of Paul's churches.

The Cover-Up's Echoes

The Hasmonean cover-up, burning Zadokite records, aimed to erase "the Way's" roots, but Paul's conversion thwarted that. By embracing the Essenes' teachings, he preserved their legacy, even as the Pharisees rebuilt Judaism after the Temple's fall in 70 AD. His letters, like Ephesians 2:19-20, tie believers to the "household of God... built upon the foundation of the apostles and prophets", echoing the Essenes' prophetic hope.

The Next Clue: The War Scroll

Paul's shift from persecutor to disciple was huge, but what about the Essenes' end-time vision? Their *War Scroll* describes a battle between the "Sons of Light" and "Sons of Darkness," a theme John and Yeshua echoed. How did this shape the 3000's faith? That's our next lead, and it's going to reveal the spiritual war behind Acts 2.

Chapter 12: The War Scroll - Sons of Light vs. Sons of Darkness

We're diving into the thick of this mystery, and this chapter's like finding a battle plan in the middle of a detective case. We've traced the Zadokite priesthood from Sinai, through their exile after the Maccabean revolt, to the Essenes who preserved their faith in Qumran and "Damascus," expecting two Messiahs—John the Baptist and Yeshua. We've seen how the 3000 believers in Acts 2 were Essenes, primed by their solar calendar, beliefs, and John's preaching. Last chapter, Paul's conversion showed how he went from persecuting "the Way" to spreading its message, influenced by Essene teachings. Now, we're cracking open one of the most intense Dead Sea Scrolls: the *War Scroll*. This text lays out a cosmic battle between the "Sons of Light" and the "Sons of Darkness," a vision that echoes John the Baptist's fiery preaching and ties directly to the 3000's readiness for Acts 2. We'll uncover how this spiritual war shaped the early believers. Get ready—this is where the stakes get sky-high!

The War Scroll: A Blueprint for Battle

The *War Scroll*, found among the Dead Sea Scrolls at Qumran, is like a script for an end-time showdown. Written around the 1st century BC, it describes a 40-year war where the "Sons of Light"—the Essenes and their allies—battle the "Sons of Darkness," led by the corrupt priests, Pharisees, and their Gentile backers, called the "Kittim" (likely Romans).

The War Scroll isn't just about swords and shields; it's a spiritual war for God's truth, with the Essenes as the righteous remnant.

The scroll details battle formations, prayers, and God's ultimate victory, led by the two Messiahs—a priestly one and a kingly one.

The scroll opens with a bold declaration: "For the Sons of Light against the lot of the Sons of Darkness, the army of Belial" (1QM, 1:1). Belial is a demonic figure, the leader of evil forces. The Essenes saw themselves as God's army, guided by the Holy Spirit and the Zadokite priesthood, fighting to restore the true covenant. This wasn't just a future hope; it shaped their daily lives, as they prepared for a divine reckoning.

John's Preaching: Echoes of the War Scroll

Now, let's connect this to John the Baptist. His preaching in the wilderness was like a trumpet blast from the *War Scroll*. In Matthew 3:7-10, he confronts the Pharisees and Sadducees: "O generation of vipers, who hath warned you to flee from the wrath to come? Bring forth therefore fruits meet for repentance… And now also the axe is laid unto the root of the trees." That's not just tough talk; it's the language of spiritual warfare, pitting the righteous against the corrupt. John's preaching was straight out of the War Scroll—calling out the Sons of Darkness and preparing the Sons of Light for the Messiah.

John's call to repentance and baptism mirrors the *War Scroll*'s emphasis on purification. The scroll describes ritual cleansing before battle, much like John's baptism in the Jordan to prepare Israel for God's kingdom (1QM, 14:2-5), he was rallying the faithful for the coming war. His warning of "wrath to come" aligns with the scroll's prophecy of divine judgment on the Sons of Darkness.

The Sons of Light: The Essenes and the 3,000

The *War Scroll* calls the Essenes "Sons of Light," a term tied to their Zadokite roots. The *Damascus Document* says, "The sons of Zadok who kept the charge of the sanctuary" (CD, 3:21-4:2), linking them to the righteous priesthood. This matches the early believers in Acts 2, who were called "the Way", a term the Essenes used for themselves (Isaiah 35:8). The 3,000 were likely the Sons of Light, trained by the War Scroll to see the world as a battle between God's truth and corruption.

When Peter preached at Shavuot, quoting Joel—"I will pour out of my Spirit upon all flesh" (Acts 2:17)—it resonated with the *War Scroll*'s vision of God's Spirit empowering the faithful (1QM, 12:9). The 3,000's response—repentance, baptism, and communal living (Acts 2:38, 44-45)—mirrors the scroll's call for purity and unity among the Sons of Light. They saw themselves as God's army, ready for the Messianic age John and Yeshua ushered in.

The Sons of Darkness: The Corrupt Opposition

Who were the Sons of Darkness? The *War Scroll* names the corrupt Temple priests, Pharisees, and their Gentile allies, like the Romans. This matches John's targets—the Pharisees and Sadducees, whom he called "vipers" for their hypocrisy and false traditions (Matthew 3:7). The scroll's "Kittim" likely refers to the Romans, who backed Herod and the corrupt priesthood. I argue this was a clash between Hebrew purity and foreign corruption, a theme John echoed.

Yeshua picked up this fight, too. In Matthew 23:13, he says, "Woe unto you, scribes and Sadducees, hypocrites! for ye shut up the kingdom of heaven against men" (HTV). His cleansing of the Temple was a direct challenge to the Sons of Darkness, fulfilling the *War Scroll*'s call to purify worship. The 3,000, steeped in this vision, saw Yeshua's actions as the kingly Messiah's strike against evil.

The Acts 2 Connection: The War Scroll's Legacy

Here's the big clue for our mystery: the *War Scroll* shaped the 3,000's mindset. They weren't just random Jews at Shavuot; they were Essenes, trained to see the world as a battleground. Their solar calendar put them in Jerusalem on the right day (Chapter 5), and their belief in two Messiahs—John and Yeshua—made Peter's sermon a rallying cry (Acts 2:22-24). The scroll's emphasis on the Holy Spirit matched the outpouring they experienced, and their communal living reflected the scroll's call for unity (1QM, 13:7-8).

The War Scroll prepared the Essenes for Acts 2. They saw John's preaching as the battle's opening shot and Yeshua's resurrection as the victory. The 3000 were the Sons of Light, joining the fight. Their baptism was like enlisting in God's army, ready to spread "the Way."

The Cover-Up's Shadow

The Hasmonean cover-up, burning Zadokite records, tried to erase this vision, but the Essenes hid their scrolls in Qumran's caves. The *War Scroll* survived, preserving the truth about the spiritual war. The Pharisees, rewriting Judaism after 70 AD, ignored this, but the 3000 carried it forward.

The Next Clue: The Holy Spirit's Role

The *War Scroll* highlights the Holy Spirit's power in the battle, a theme central to Acts 2. How did the Essenes' belief in the Spirit shape the 3,000's response? That's our next lead, and it's going to reveal the divine fire behind their faith.

Chapter 13: The Holy Spirit - Essene Belief and the Fire of Acts 2

We're closing in on the climax of this mystery, and this chapter's like a spotlight illuminating the heart of it all. We've followed the Zadokite priesthood from Sinai, through their exile, to the Essenes who preserved their faith in Qumran and "Damascus," expecting two Messiahs—John the Baptist and Yeshua. We've seen how the 3000 believers in Acts 2, were primed by their Zadok solar calendar, their *War Scroll*'s battle cry, and John's preaching. Now, we're diving into the spark that set it all ablaze: the Holy Spirit. The outpouring in Acts 2 wasn't just a dramatic moment; it was the fulfillment of Essene beliefs about God's Spirit, rooted in their scrolls and Zadokite heritage. We'll uncover how the Essenes' view of the Holy Spirit made the 3000 ready for that Shavuot miracle. Get ready—this is where the divine fire meets human faith!

The Holy Spirit in Essene Belief: A Guiding Light

For the Essenes, the Holy Spirit wasn't just a vague idea; it was central to their faith. Their Dead Sea Scrolls, like the *Community Rule* (1QS), describe the Spirit as God's tool for cleansing, guiding, and empowering the faithful. The scroll says, "By His truth He will purify all human deeds, and by the spirit of holiness He will cleanse them from all wicked actions" (1QS, 4:20-21). This wasn't about rituals alone; it was about God's Spirit transforming hearts to live out the pure Torah. The Essenes believed the Holy Spirit would lead them to truth and prepare them for the Messiahs. It was their lifeline in exile.

This belief came from their Zadokite roots. Ezekiel 36:26-27, a key text for the Essenes, says, "A new heart also will I give you, and a new spirit will I put within you… And I will put my spirit within you, and cause you to walk in my statutes." The Essenes saw themselves as the remnant receiving this Spirit, keeping the covenant pure after the Hasmonean betrayal (Chapter 3). Unlike the Pharisees, who leaned on their Oral Torah, or the Sadducees, who denied the Spirit altogether, the Essenes expected a divine outpouring to mark the Messianic age.

The War Scroll: The Spirit in Battle

The *War Scroll*, which we explored last chapter, ties the Holy Spirit to the cosmic battle between the Sons of Light and Sons of Darkness. It says, "By the Holy Spirit of the truth… the Sons of Light shall prevail" (1QM, 13:9-10). The Essenes believed God's Spirit would empower them to overcome evil, led by the priestly and kingly Messiahs. This wasn't just future talk; it shaped their daily lives in Qumran, where they practiced ritual purity and communal living to stay ready for the Spirit's work.

The War Scroll shows the Essenes saw the Holy Spirit as their strength in the fight for God's kingdom. When Acts 2 happened, it was like their prophecy coming true. This belief set them apart, making them open to the dramatic events of Shavuot.

John's Preaching: A Call to Spiritual Renewal

John the Baptist, the priestly Messiah (Chapter 7), was steeped in this Essene mindset. His preaching in the wilderness wasn't just about repentance; it was about preparing for the Spirit. Matthew 3:11 says, "I indeed baptize you with water unto repentance: but he that cometh after me is mightier than I… he shall baptize you with the Holy Spirit, and with fire." That's Essene language—cleansing now, but a greater Spirit-led transformation to come. The *Damascus Document* calls for purification to prepare for God's kingdom (CD, 6:17-18), and John's baptism in the Jordan was a living example, drawing crowds including Essenes.

John's message was the Essenes' message: get ready, because the Spirit's coming to change everything. He primed the 3,000 for Acts 2. The Essenes, expecting this outpouring, saw John as their "Teacher of Righteousness," preparing them for Yeshua's kingdom.

Acts 2: The Spirit's Outpouring

Now, let's get to the main event: Acts 2. The scene is Jerusalem, Shavuot, around 30 AD. The apostles are gathered, likely with Essene believers following the solar calendar. Acts 2:1-4 describes it: "And when the day of Pentecost was fully come, they were all with one accord in one place. And suddenly there came a sound from heaven as of a rushing mighty wind… And there appeared unto them cloven tongues like as of fire… And they were all filled with the Holy Spirit." Peter quotes Joel 2:28-29: "I will pour out of my Spirit upon all flesh: and your sons and your daughters shall prophesy."

This was the moment the Essenes had been waiting for.

The *Community Rule*'s promise of the Spirit cleansing the faithful (1QS, 4:20-21) came alive. The tongues of fire and speaking in languages matched their expectation of a divine outpouring. The 3000, likely Essenes, responded instantly, getting baptized and joining "the Way." Why? Because their scrolls had prepared them for this exact moment. The Holy Spirit in Acts 2 was the Essenes' prophecy fulfilled. They were ready, unlike the Pharisees or Sadducees.

The Acts 2 Connection: Why the 3000 Responded

Here's the big clue for our mystery: the Essenes' belief in the Holy Spirit made the 3,000 uniquely ready for Acts 2. The Pharisees, focused on their Oral Torah, didn't emphasize the Spirit. The Sadducees flat-out denied it (Josephus, *Antiquities*, Book 18, Chapter 1). But the Essenes, rooted in Zadokite teachings, saw the Spirit as God's power to renew the covenant. When Peter preached, "Repent, and be baptized every one of you in the name of Messiah Yeshua for the remission of sins, and ye shall receive the gift of the Holy Spirit" (Acts 2:38), it was like a key turning in a lock for them.

Their communal living, described in Acts 2:44-45—"And all that believed were together, and had all things common"—mirrored the *Community Rule*'s call for sharing everything (1QS, 1:11-12). Their readiness came from years of Qumran's discipline, John's baptism, and the *War Scroll*'s vision of the Spirit-led battle. Yeshua's teachings, like "The Spirit of the Lord is upon me" (Luke 4:18, KJV, quoting Isaiah 61:1), and his promise of the Spirit in John 16:13, reinforced their hope.

The Cover-Up's Failure

The Hasmonean cover-up, burning Zadokite records, tried to erase this spiritual vision, but the Essenes preserved it in their scrolls. The Pharisees' lunar calendar and traditions sidelined the Spirit, but the 3,000 carried the Essene flame forward, spreading "the Way" (Acts 9:2, KJV).

The Next Clue: Restoration Themes

The Holy Spirit's outpouring was about more than miracles; it was about restoring God's covenant, as Isaiah 35 and Malachi 4 promised. How did the Essenes' hope for restoration shape the 3,000's faith? That's our next lead, and it's going to tie this mystery to the bigger picture of God's plan.

Chapter 14: Restoration and the Elijah Connection

We're nearing the end of this detective journey, and this chapter's like finding the final piece of a puzzle that makes everything click. We've traced the Zadokite priesthood from Sinai, through their exile after the Maccabean revolt, to the Essenes who preserved their faith in Qumran and "Damascus," expecting two Messiahs—John the Baptist and Yeshua. The 3,000 believers in Acts 2, likely Essenes, were primed by their solar calendar, the *War Scroll*'s battle cry, and their belief in the Holy Spirit. Last chapter, we saw how the Spirit's outpouring fulfilled their hopes, tying directly to their scrolls. Now, we're diving into the restoration themes in Isaiah 35 and Malachi 4, which the Essenes cherished, and their connection to Elijah's promised return. These prophecies fueled their hope for a renewed covenant and pointed to John the Baptist as Elijah's successor, preparing the 3,000 for Acts 2. We'll uncover how these restoration promises shaped the early believers. Get ready—this is where the mystery ties into God's grand plan!

Restoration in Isaiah 35: A Highway for the Redeemed

The Essenes weren't just waiting for a fight; they were longing for restoration—a return to the pure covenant God gave at Sinai. Isaiah 35 was one of their key texts, painting a vivid picture of this hope. The chapter opens with a vision of renewal: "The wilderness and the solitary place shall be glad for them; and the desert shall rejoice, and blossom as the rose" (Isaiah 35:1). For the Essenes, living in the Qumran wilderness, this was personal—God would transform their exile into glory.

The chapter's climax is verse 8: "And a highway shall be there, and a way, and it shall be called The way of holiness; the unclean shall not pass over it; but it shall be for those: the wayfaring men, though fools, shall not err therein." This "way of holiness" wasn't just a path; it was a lifestyle, the Essenes' identity as "the Way" (1QS, 9:17-18). Isaiah 35 was the Essenes' anthem. They called themselves 'the Way,' believing God would restore Israel through a holy remnant. This matches Acts 9:2, where early believers are called "the Way", linking the 3000 to the Essenes.

Isaiah 35:10 seals the promise: "And the ransomed of the Lord shall return, and come to Zion with songs and everlasting joy upon their heads." The Essenes saw themselves as that remnant, returning to Zion—Jerusalem—for feasts like Shavuot, ready for God's kingdom. Their solar calendar ensured they were there on the right day, as we saw in Chapter 5, when the Spirit fell in Acts 2:1-4.

Malachi 4: The Elijah Promise

Malachi 4 takes this restoration to another level, tying it to Elijah. The chapter ends with a prophecy: "Behold, I will send you Elijah the prophet before the coming of the great and dreadful day of the Lord: And he shall turn the heart of the fathers to the children, and the heart of the children to their fathers, lest I come and smite the earth with a curse" (Malachi 4:5-6). The Essenes took this seriously, expecting Elijah or an Elijah-like figure to herald the Messianic age. Their Dead Sea Scroll 4Q76, tweaking Malachi 3:1-2 to say "them", showed they linked this to their two-Messiah hope—priestly and kingly.

John the Baptist was that Elijah figure. Luke 1:17 says the angel Gabriel told Zachariah, John's father, that his son would go "in the spirit and power of Elias, to turn the hearts of the fathers to the children, and the disobedient to the wisdom of the just; to make ready a people prepared for the Lord." This echoes Malachi 4:6 word for word. The Essenes saw John as Elijah's successor, the priestly Messiah preparing for Yeshua. His wilderness preaching was their restoration signal.

John's call to repentance (Matthew 3:2) and baptism (Matthew 3:6) fulfilled Malachi's promise, turning hearts back to the covenant. The Essenes, steeped in this prophecy, flocked to him, as Mark 1:5 says: "And there went out unto him all the land of Judaea, and they of Jerusalem, and were all baptized of him in the river of Jordan." This set the stage for Acts 2, where the 3000—likely Essenes—were ready for Peter's message.

The Elijah Connection: John as the Forerunner

The Essenes' belief in Elijah's return tied directly to their Zadokite roots. As we saw in Chapter 7, John's Aaronic lineage made him a perfect candidate for the priestly Messiah (Luke 1:5). His wilderness life, among Essenes at Qumran, and his fiery preaching against the "vipers" (Matthew 3:7) matched their *War Scroll*'s battle cry (1QM, 1:1). The *Damascus Document* calls for a *"Teacher of Righteousness"* to guide the remnant (CD, 1:11), preparing the Essenes for Yeshua's kingdom.

When the Pharisees asked who John was, he replied, "I am a voice of one crying in the wilderness - make straight The Way of the Lord." (Isaiah 40:3) This was the anthem of the Essenes.

Yeshua himself confirmed this. In Matthew 11:14, he says of John, "And if you want to receive it (the kingdom of heaven), this (John the Baptist) is *like unto* Elijah, who has been prepared to come." (HTV). The Essenes, unlike the Pharisees or Sadducees, were ready to receive it. Their scrolls, like the *Community Rule* (1QS, 9:11), expected a prophet like Elijah alongside the Messiahs, restoring the covenant. John's baptism wasn't just a ritual; it was a call to renew the "way of holiness" from Isaiah 35, aligning with the Essenes' mission.

The Acts 2 Connection: Restoration Fulfilled

Here's the big clue for our mystery: the restoration themes in Isaiah 35 and Malachi 4, centered on Elijah, made the 3000 ready for Acts 2. The Essenes saw themselves as the "ransomed of the Lord" (Isaiah 35:10), gathered in Jerusalem for Shavuot on their solar calendar. When the Holy Spirit fell— "a sound from heaven as of a rushing mighty wind" (Acts 2:2)—it was the restoration they'd been waiting for. Peter's sermon, quoting Joel about the Spirit (Acts 2:17), and his call to "repent, and be baptized" echoed John's Elijah-like mission, turning hearts to God. The 3000's response—baptism and communal living—reflected the Essenes' lifestyle, shaped by Isaiah's "way of holiness" and Malachi's call for renewal.

The Essenes were waiting for Elijah to restore the covenant.

John was that Elijah, and Acts 2 was the payoff for their faith. Their belief in the Holy Spirit, as seen in the *Community Rule* (1QS, 4:20-21), matched the fire and tongues of Acts 2.

The Cover-Up's Defeat

The Hasmonean cover-up, burning Zadokite records, tried to erase these prophecies, but the Essenes preserved them in their scrolls. The Pharisees' Oral Torah ignored Elijah's role, but the 3,000 carried the restoration hope forward, spreading "the Way".

The Final Clue: The Messianic Faith

Isaiah 35 and Malachi 4 point to a restored covenant, but how did the 3,000's Essene faith shape the early Messianic movement? That's our final lead, and it's going to show why their story isn't just history—it's the root of our faith today.

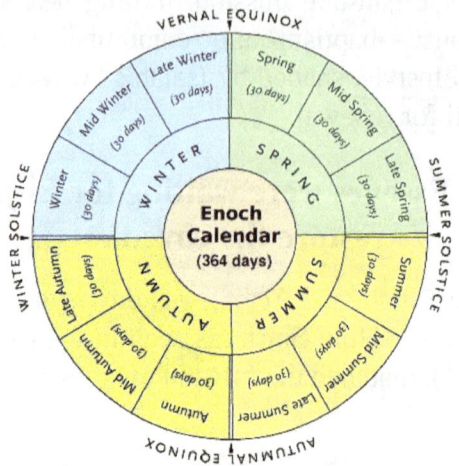

Chapter 15: From Sinai to Qumran to Today - The Restoration Continues

This is like standing on a mountaintop, seeing the whole landscape come into view. We've traced the Zadokite priesthood from their covenant at Sinai, through their exile after the Maccabean revolt, to the Essenes who preserved their faith in Qumran and "Damascus," expecting two Messiahs—John the Baptist and Yeshua. The 3,000 believers in Acts 2, were Essenes, primed by their solar calendar, the *War Scroll*'s battle cry, their belief in the Holy Spirit, and restoration prophecies like Isaiah 35 and Malachi 4. Now, we're pulling all these threads together to explore the end-time implications of this journey. The Essenes' faith wasn't just a historical footnote; it's a call to restore the pure covenant today, connecting Sinai to Qumran to our modern faith. Get ready—this is where the mystery points to our future!

The Essene Vision: A Restored Covenant

The Essenes weren't just hiding in the desert; they were preserving a vision of restoration that started at Sinai. There, God gave

Chapter 15: End-time Implications, Tying Sinai to Qumran to Today's Faith

Israel the Torah and a priesthood to guard it (Exodus 28:1). The Zadokites, as we saw in Chapter 2, were the "righteous ones" who kept this covenant pure under David and Solomon, using a 364-day solar calendar to align with God's *moedim* (appointed times). After their exile in the Maccabean revolt (Chapter 3), they formed the Essene communities, like Qumran and "Damascus," to await the Messiahs who would restore Israel (Chapter 10).

The *Damascus Document* calls them the "sons of Zadok" who "kept the charge of the sanctuary" (CD, 3:21-4:2), and their *Community Rule* envisions a renewed covenant led by the Holy Spirit (1QS, 4:20-21). Isaiah 35:8's "way of holiness" and Malachi 4:5-6's promise of Elijah's return fueled their hope for a return to God's original plan (Chapter 14). The Essenes believed God would restore the covenant through the Messiahs, bringing back the purity of Sinai. Acts 2 was the start.

Acts 2: The Restoration Begins

The 3,000 believers in Acts 2 were the first fruits of this restoration. On Shavuot, following the Essenes' solar calendar (Chapter 5), the Holy Spirit fell: "And suddenly there came a sound from heaven as of a rushing mighty wind... And they were all filled with the Holy Spirit." Peter's sermon, quoting Joel 2:28-29 about the Spirit's outpouring (Acts 2:17), and his call to "repent, and be baptized" echoed the Essenes' expectations. Their communal living—"all that believed were together, and had all things common"—mirrored Qumran's practices (1QS, 1:11-12).

This wasn't a new religion; it was a return to the covenant,

with John as the Elijah-like priestly Messiah (Chapter 7) and Yeshua as the Davidic kingly Messiah (Chapter 8). The *War Scroll*'s battle of the Sons of Light against the Sons of Darkness (1QM, 1:1) came alive as the 3,000 joined "the Way", fighting for God's truth against corruption. Acts 2 was the Essenes' restoration dream coming true. The 3,000 were the remnant, carrying the torch.

End-Time Implications: The Restoration Continues

But the story doesn't end in Acts 2. The Essenes' vision, rooted in Isaiah 35 and Malachi 4, points to an ongoing restoration that's relevant today. Isaiah 35:10 promises, "The ransomed of the Lord shall return, and come to Zion with songs and everlasting joy." The Essenes saw this as a future return to God's kingdom, and Acts 2 was just the beginning. The *War Scroll* envisions a final victory where the Sons of Light, empowered by the Spirit, defeat evil (1QM, 13:9-10). This hasn't fully happened yet—it's an end-time promise.

The Essenes' faith is a blueprint for today. We're called to restore the pure Torah, the solar calendar, and the Spirit-led life, just as they did. The Hasmonean cover-up, burning Zadokite records, tried to bury this vision, but the Dead Sea Scrolls preserved it. Modern believers can learn from the Essenes by rejecting man-made traditions, like the Pharisees' Oral Torah, and returning to God's written word, as Yeshua taught in Matthew 5:17-18: "I came not that I might fulfill (complete or end) but rather that I might fill (the Torah) to overflowing" (HTV).

The Elijah Connection Today

Malachi 4:5-6's promise of Elijah turning "the heart of the fathers to the children, and the heart of the children to their fathers" is still alive. John fulfilled this as the priestly Messiah, but the spirit of Elijah—calling for repentance and covenant renewal—continues. The Essenes expected a final restoration, and Revelation 11:3-4 echoes this with the "two witnesses," reminiscent of Zechariah 4:14's "two anointed ones." Are we, today, called to be part of this remnant, preparing for the Messiah's return?

The Elijah spirit is about restoring God's truth in the last days. The Essenes show us how—live simply, follow the Torah, and trust the Spirit. The 3000's faith, rooted in Essene practices, challenges us to reject corruption and embrace the "way of holiness" (Isaiah 35:8).

Tying Sinai to Today: A Call to Action

The journey from Sinai to Qumran to Acts 2 is a straight line to our time. The Zadokites' covenant-keeping, the Essenes' exile, and the 3,000's response show a pattern: God preserves a remnant to restore His truth. The solar calendar, the Holy Spirit, and the two-Messiah prophecy aren't just history—they're a call to return to God's original design. In *Sons of Zion vs Sons of Greece*, I argue this is a battle against foreign corruption, like the Babylonian lunar calendar. Today's faith restoration means embracing the Torah, the Spirit, and the Messianic hope, just as the 3000 did.

The 3000's story isn't just about the past; it's a mirror for us.

Are we living as the Sons of Light, ready for the final restoration? As Peter said in Acts 3:19, "Repent therefore, and be converted, that your sins may be blotted out, when the times of refreshing shall come from the presence of the Lord." That's the Essene vision, and it's ours to carry forward.

The Failed Plans

The Hasmonean cover-up failed. The Essenes' scrolls, hidden in caves, outlasted the destruction, revealing God's plan. The 3000 were the first to live it, and we're called to finish it. The mystery of Acts 2 isn't just who those believers were—it's what their faith means for us. Let's pick up their torch and run.

Chapter 16: The Essenes' Influence on Early Christianity

We've been on a wild ride, piecing together the mystery of the 3,000 believers in Acts 2, and we've pinned them as likely Essenes, heirs of the Zadokite priesthood from Sinai, exiled after the Maccabean revolt, and thriving in Qumran and "Damascus." Their solar calendar, expectation of two Messiahs—John the Baptist and Yeshua—and faith in the Holy Spirit made them ready for Peter's sermon and the Spirit's outpouring. But their story doesn't end at Shavuot; it's like a river flowing into the early Christian movement, shaping its practices, theology, and mission. In this chapter, we're digging into how the Essenes' legacy left an indelible mark on the early church, from communal living to spiritual warfare to the spread of "the Way." We'll uncover how these desert dwellers influenced Christianity's first steps. Get ready—this clue shows the 3000 weren't just a moment in time; they were the spark for a global faith!

Communal Living: From Qumran to the Early Church

Let's start with one of the most striking parallels: the way the early Christians lived. Acts 2:44-45 paints a vivid picture: "And all that believed were together, and had all things common; and sold their possessions and goods, and parted them to all men, as every man had need." Sound familiar? It's practically a page out of the Essenes' playbook. The *Community Rule* from Qumran mandates, "All who submit freely to His truth will bring their knowledge, their strength, and their wealth into the community of God" (1QS, 1:11-12). At Qumran, the Essenes shared everything—food, resources, even their lives—rejecting the materialism of the Sadducees and the individualism of the Pharisees.

The 3000 in Acts 2 were Essenes because their communal lifestyle was second nature to them. They brought Qumran's model to the early church. This wasn't a one-off; Acts 4:32 reinforces it: "Neither said any of them that ought of the things which he possessed was his own; but they had all things common." This communal spirit spread to other Christian communities, like those Paul oversaw, who collected offerings for the poor (1 Corinthians 16:1-3). The Essenes' rejection of wealth, rooted in their Zadokite call to holiness (Ezekiel 44:23), became a cornerstone of early Christian ethics, setting them apart in a greedy Roman world.

The Holy Spirit: A Shared Expectation

The Essenes' belief in the Holy Spirit as a transformative force was another gift to the early church. The *Community Rule* declares, "By the spirit of holiness He will cleanse them from all wicked actions" (1QS, 4:20-21), echoing Ezekiel 36:27: "I will put my spirit within you, and cause you to walk in my statutes" (KJV). This expectation of a divine outpouring primed the 3000 for Acts 2, when "they were all filled with the Holy Ghost, and began to speak with other tongues" (Acts 2:4). Peter's quote from Joel—"I will pour out of my Spirit upon all flesh" (Acts 2:17)—was like a signal flare for the Essenes, who'd been waiting for this moment.

This focus on the Spirit didn't fade. Paul, after his Damascus conversion (Chapter 11), taught that "the manifestation of the Spirit is given to every man to profit withal" (1 Corinthians 12:7), listing gifts like prophecy and healing—ideas resonant with the Essenes' *Hymns Scroll* (1QH, 6:12), which praises the Spirit's role in renewing the faithful. The Essenes' view of the Spirit as a guide and purifier shaped the early church's understanding of spiritual gifts. Unlike the Sadducees, who denied the Spirit, or the Pharisees, who downplayed it, the early Christians embraced a vibrant pneumatology, thanks to the Essenes' influence through the 3000.

Messianic Theology: Two Messiahs in Christian Thought

The Essenes' expectation of two Messiahs—a priestly one from Aaron and a kingly one from David (1QSa; Zechariah 4:14)—left a subtle but profound mark on Christian theology. While mainstream Judaism awaited a single Davidic warrior, the Essenes saw a priestly forerunner preparing for a kingly ruler, fulfilled by John the Baptist and Yeshua (Chapters 7 and 8). This dual framework appears in early Christian texts. Hebrews 7:17 calls Yeshua a "priest for ever after the order of Melchizedek", blending priestly and kingly roles in a way that echoes Essene thought, which saw Melchizedek as a divine figure in scrolls like 11Q13.

Yeshua himself affirmed John's role, saying, "this (John the Baptist) is *like unto* Elijah, who has been prepared to come." (Matthew 11:14, HTV), tying John to Malachi 4:5's prophecy (Chapter 14). The early church, influenced by Essene converts, carried this idea forward, seeing Yeshua as the kingly Messiah who fulfilled the Torah (Matthew 5:17). The Essenes' two-Messiah prophecy gave the early church a richer view of Yeshua's role, balancing priestly and kingly aspects. This set Christianity apart from Pharisaic Judaism, which rejected Yeshua's priestly claims.

Chapter 16: The Essenes' Influence on Early Christianity

Opposition to Corruption: A Shared Battle

The Essenes' fight against the corrupt Hasmonean priesthood, as seen in the *Damascus Document* (CD, 1:12), resonated in the early church's stance against religious hypocrisy. Yeshua's cleansing of the Temple—"It is written, My house shall be called the house of prayer; but ye have made it a den of thieves" (Matthew 21:13)—mirrors the *War Scroll*'s battle cry against the Sons of Darkness (1QM, 1:1; Chapter 12). Peter's confrontation with Ananias and Sapphira, who lied about their offerings (Acts 5:3-5), reflects the Essenes' demand for purity, as in "Let no man lie in matters of justice" (1QS, 6:1).

This opposition wasn't just about rules; it was about restoring God's covenant,

as Isaiah 35:8's "way of holiness" promised (Chapter 14). The early church, led by Essene-like believers, challenged the Pharisees' Oral Torah and the Sadducees' materialism, much as John called them "vipers" (Matthew 3:7). This was a clash of Hebrew purity against foreign corruption, a fight the early Christians inherited.

The Gentile Mission: An Essene Seed

The Essenes' vision wasn't limited to Israel. The *Community Rule* hints at a broader mission: "To prepare the way of the Lord in the wilderness" (1QS, 8:14, citing Isaiah 40:3). While they focused on Israel's remnant, this openness laid groundwork for the church's Gentile outreach. Acts 10, where Peter baptizes Cornelius, a Gentile, after a vision, reflects this shift. Paul, post-Damascus, took this further, preaching to Gentiles (Galatians 1:16). "The Essenes' emphasis on the Torah's universal truth, without Pharisaic additions, may have inspired Paul's gospel of faith. Romans 3:31—"Do we then make void the law through faith? God forbid: yes, we establish the law"—echoes the Essenes' Torah-centric faith.

Archaeological and Textual Evidence

Qumran's ruins—*mikvahs*, a dining hall, a scriptorium—show a community geared for spiritual renewal, influencing Christian practices like baptism and communal meals. The scrolls' survival, despite Hasmonean attempts to erase Zadokite records, ensured their ideas reached the church. Early Christian texts like the *Didache*, with rules for baptism and prayer, resemble Essene practices in the *Community Rule*. Scholars like Geza Vermes note parallels between Qumran's communal life and the Jerusalem church under James, Yeshua's brother, who upheld Torah observance (Acts 15:20-21).

The Acts 2 Connection and Beyond

The 3,000 in Acts 2, likely Essenes, were the bridge between Qumran and the church. Their faith in the Spirit, two Messiahs, and the Torah shaped early Christianity's identity. James' leadership in Jerusalem, emphasizing "abstaining from pollutions of idols" (Acts 15:20), reflects Essene purity. Paul's churches, with their collections for the poor (Romans 15:26), carried forward Qumran's communal ethos. The Essenes' legacy lived on, spreading "the Way" from Jerusalem to the world (Acts 1:8).

Chapter 17: The Essene Call Today - Restoring the Covenant

We've chased this mystery from the burning sands of Sinai to the caves of Qumran, from the fiery preaching of John the Baptist to the Spirit-filled Shavuot of Acts 2, where 3,000 believers—likely Essenes—joined "the Way." We've seen the Zadokite priesthood guard God's covenant, their exile after the Maccabean revolt, and the Essenes' preservation of their faith through a solar calendar, two-Messiah prophecy, and trust in the Holy Spirit. Their story, preserved in the Dead Sea Scrolls, fueled the early church and the 3,000's response to Peter's sermon. But this isn't just a tale of ancient scrolls and desert communes—it's a living call to restore God's covenant today. In this final chapter, we'll explore how the Essenes' faith inspires modern movements, from Messianic Judaism to biblical calendar revivals, and challenges us to live as Sons of Light in a world of darkness. Let's uncover how the Essenes' legacy points to a faith restoration now. The trail ends here, but the mission begins—let's dive in!

Rediscovering the Torah: A Return to the Written Word

The Essenes were fierce about one thing: sticking to God's written Torah, free from human additions. They rejected the Pharisees' Oral Torah, which Yeshua also criticized: "You despise the commandment of God for the sake of your traditions." (Matthew 15:6). Their *Community Rule* demanded living by "the law of Moses according to all that was revealed" (1QS, 5:8). This resonates today with Messianic Jewish and Hebrew Roots movements, which call believers back to the Torah as the schoolmaster of faith.

The Essenes show us that God's Word, not man's rules, is the standard.

Modern believers can learn from them to study the Torah without extra baggage. Groups like *First Fruits of Zion* and the *Messianic Jewish Alliance* emphasize Yeshua's role as the Torah's fulfillment, echoing his words: "I came not that I might fulfill (complete or end) but rather that I might fill (the Torah) to overflowing" (Matthew 5:17). This isn't about legalism; it's about embracing God's instructions, from Sabbath-observing to loving your neighbor (Leviticus 19:18), as the Essenes did. For today's believers, this means digging into scripture, questioning traditions, and living out the covenant as the 3000 did in Acts 2:42-45.

Reviving the Solar Calendar: God's Appointed Times

The Essenes' 364-day solar calendar, rooted in the Book of Enoch and detailed in Qumran's *Calendrical Texts* (4Q320-321), kept God's feasts (*moedim*) on fixed dates, unlike the Pharisees' shifting lunar calendar (Chapter 5). This ensured they were in Jerusalem for Shavuot when the Spirit fell. Restoring the solar calendar is about honoring God's timing, aligning our worship with creation's rhythm.

Today, groups like the Enoch Calendar movement and certain Messianic communities are revisiting this calendar, arguing it reflects Genesis 1:14's "lights in the firmament... for seasons."

The lunar calendar, influenced by Babylonian exile, disrupted the Zadokite system, shifting feasts like Shavuot by weeks. Modern believers are studying scrolls like 4Q321 to fix Passover, Shavuot, and Sukkot on consistent dates, aiming to worship as God intended. This revival isn't just academic—it's a call to align with the Essenes' precision, preparing us for spiritual moments like Acts 2, when God's timing meets human readiness.

The Holy Spirit: A Modern Outpouring

The Essenes' trust in the Holy Spirit as a guide and purifier, seen in the *Community Rule*—"By the spirit of holiness He will cleanse them" (1QS, 4:20-21)—primed the 3,000 for Acts 2's "tongues like as of fire" (Acts 2:3-4). Their *Hymns Scroll* praises the Spirit's renewal (1QH, 6:12), a theme echoed in Ezekiel 36:27: "I will put my spirit within you." Today, charismatic and renewal movements mirror this, seeking a fresh outpouring of the Spirit.

The Essenes' expectation of the Spirit is a model for us. Acts 2 wasn't a one-time event—it's a pattern for revival. From Pentecostal churches to Messianic congregations, believers pray for spiritual gifts, like prophecy and healing (1 Corinthians 12:7-11), reflecting the Essenes' openness to God's power. This call challenges us to seek the Spirit's guidance, as the 3,000 did, living boldly in a world that often denies the divine.

The Elijah Spirit: Restoring Hearts

Malachi 4:5-6's promise—"I will send you Elijah the prophet… to turn the heart of the fathers to the children."—was fulfilled by John the Baptist (Matthew 11:14), but its spirit lives on. The Essenes saw John as their "Teacher of Righteousness" (CD, 1:11), preparing for Yeshua through repentance and baptism (Chapter 7). Today, this Elijah spirit calls believers to restore relationships and covenant faithfulness.

The Elijah spirit is about healing families and communities, turning us back to God's ways. Modern ministries, like those focusing on family reconciliation or Torah-based ethics, embody this, urging believers to mend broken bonds, as the 3,000 did in their communal living (Acts 2:44-45). Revelation 11:3-4's "two witnesses" suggest a future Elijah-like role, inspiring us to prepare for the Messiah's return by living out the Essenes' call to holiness (Isaiah 35:8).

Archaeological and Cultural Impact

The 1947 discovery of the Dead Sea Scrolls sparked a global fascination with the Essenes. Qumran's ruins—*mikvahs*, dining halls, and scriptorium—are pilgrimage sites for those seeking biblical roots. Scholars like Geza Vermes and books like Hugh Schonfield's *The Essene Odyssey* highlight their influence, from baptism to communal living. The scrolls are God's gift to our generation, revealing the Essenes' faith as a guide for today. Museums displaying Qumran artifacts, like the Israel Museum, and online resources make their legacy accessible, inspiring believers to study their practices.

Modern Messianic festivals, like Sukkot gatherings, often draw on Essene-inspired themes of purity and community. Archaeological debates, such as whether Qumran was solely Essene or a broader sect's home, keep their story alive, pushing us to dig deeper into their covenant-keeping mission.

The Call to Be Sons of Light

The *War Scroll*'s battle of the Sons of Light against the Sons of Darkness (1QM, 1:1) wasn't just ancient—it's our fight. The Essenes rejected Hasmonean corruption, hiding their scrolls from destruction. Today, we face modern "Sons of Darkness"—secularism, relativism, and religious compromise. The Essenes' example—living simply, studying Torah, and trusting the Spirit—calls us to stand firm, as Yeshua did against the "den of thieves" (Matthew 21:13).

Intentional communities, like some Messianic or Anabaptist groups, mirror Qumran's model, sharing resources and prioritizing faith. The Essenes' hope for restoration, seen in Isaiah 35:10—"The ransomed of the Lord shall return"—inspires us to build lives of holiness, preparing for the Messiah's return, as Acts 3:19 urges: "Repent, therefore… that the times of refreshing shall come."

The Acts 2 Connection: A Timeless Challenge

The 3,000, likely Essenes, carried the Zadokite torch into the church, shaping its communal, Spirit-filled, Torah-centric faith (Chapter 16). Their response to Peter's sermon (Acts 2:38) challenges us to repent, embrace the Spirit, and live as a covenant community. The Essenes' legacy, preserved despite Hasmonean cover-ups, calls us to reject man-made traditions and return to Sinai's purity.

Chapter 18: The Role of Women in Essene Communities and Early Christianity

We're peeling back another layer of this mystery, like finding a hidden chapter in an ancient scroll. We've traced the Zadokite priesthood from Sinai, through their exile, to the Essenes who preserved their faith in Qumran and "Damascus," expecting two Messiahs—John the Baptist and Yeshua. The 3,000 believers in Acts 2, likely Essenes, were primed by their solar calendar, *War Scroll*'s battle cry, and hope for the Holy Spirit. We've seen their influence ripple into the early church and inspire modern faith restoration. Now, we're shining a light on a vital but often overlooked clue: the role of women in Essene communities and how their contributions shaped the early Christian movement, including those 3,000. We'll uncover how women were active partners in "the Way" and what their legacy means today. Get ready—this trail adds a new dimension to our story!

Women in Essene Communities: More Than Silent Observers

The Essenes are often pictured as an all-male, monastic sect, but that's only half the story. While some Qumran members lived celibately, the *Damascus Document* reveals that Essene communities included families, with women and children playing active roles. CD 7:6-9 mentions "wives and children" in the covenant community, and CD 14:12-16 outlines rules for women's participation in communal life, including marriage and purity laws. The Essenes weren't just a boys' club. Women were part of their mission, upholding the Torah and preparing for the Messianic age.

Archaeological evidence from Qumran supports this. Excavations uncovered female skeletal remains in the cemetery, suggesting women lived in or near the community (de Vaux, *Archaeology and the Dead Sea Scrolls*). The *Community Rule* (1QS), while focused on male leadership, doesn't exclude women, and its call for all to live by "truth and holiness" (1QS, 5:8) applies universally. Women likely participated in ritual baths (*mikvahs*), communal meals, and Torah study, mirroring the men's dedication to purity. Their role wasn't secondary—they were co-guardians of the Zadokite covenant, rooted in Ezekiel 44:15's call for the "sons of Zadok" to keep the sanctuary, a mission that included the whole community.

Women's Spiritual Contributions: Prophecy and Purity

The Essenes' belief in the Holy Spirit, seen in the *Community Rule*—"By the spirit of holiness He will cleanse them" (1QS, 4:20-21)—extended to women. The *Hymns Scroll* (1QH) includes prayers that could reflect female voices, praising God's Spirit for renewal (1QH, 6:12). Joel 2:28, quoted by Peter in Acts 2:17, promises, "Your sons and your daughters shall prophesy", a prophecy the Essenes embraced. Women in Essene communities likely had prophetic roles, inspired by the Spirit, preparing them for Acts 2's outpouring. This prophetic role tied to John the Baptist's ministry. As the Elijah-like forerunner (Matthew 11:14; Chapter 14), John drew women to his baptism, as Mark 1:5 notes: "There went out unto him all the land of Judaea, and they of Jerusalem, and were all baptized." Women, steeped in Essene teachings, would have seen his call to repentance as part of Malachi 4:6's restoration of "the heart of the fathers to the children."

Women in Acts 2 and the Early Church

The 3000 in Acts 2 weren't just men—women were there, responding to Peter's sermon: "Repent, and be baptized every one of you" (Acts 2:38). The phrase "everyone" includes women, who joined the communal life of "the Way". Acts 1:14 sets the stage, mentioning "the women, and Mary the mother of Jesus" among the disciples praying before Shavuot. These women, influenced by Essene practices, brought their commitment to purity and community to the early church.

In Acts 9:2, Paul seeks out "any of this way, whether they were men or women" to persecute, confirming women's active role in "the Way," a term tied to the Essenes (Isaiah 35:8; Chapter 10). Figures like Lydia, a seller of purple who hosted a church (Acts 16:14-15), and Priscilla, who taught Apollos (Acts 18:26), reflect Essene-like devotion to Torah and community. Women in the early church carried the Essenes' torch—living simply, teaching truth, and spreading the faith.

Women and the Two-Messiah Prophecy

The Essenes' expectation of two Messiahs—a priestly one (John) and a kingly one (Yeshua)—likely resonated with women, who saw their roles in the covenant's restoration. The *War Scroll* envisions the Sons of Light, including the whole community, fighting for God's kingdom (1QM, 1:1; Chapter 12). Women, as mothers and teachers, nurtured this hope, passing it to children, as Malachi 4:6 suggests. Mary, Yeshua's mother, embodies this, receiving the angel's prophecy (Luke 1:30-33) and standing with the disciples in Acts 1:14.

The *Damascus Document*'s rules for women's purity (CD, 15:10-12) align with early Christian practices, like baptism for all believers. Women's involvement in Essene rituals, like *mikvahs*, prefigured Christian baptism, linking them to John's ministry. Their faith in Yeshua as the kingly Messiah, fulfilling Zechariah 4:14's "two anointed ones", strengthened the early church's theology (Chapter 16).

Archaeological and Historical Clues

Qumran's *mikvahs* and communal spaces suggest women participated in daily life, as Josephus notes some Essenes married (*War of the Jews*, 2.8.13). The Dead Sea Scrolls, preserved despite Hasmonean attempts to erase Zadokite records, include texts like 4Q270, which address women's roles in marriage and community. These findings challenge the male-only stereotype, showing women as active covenant-keepers.

Early Christian texts, like the *Didache*, echo Essene rules for purity and communal living, suggesting women's influence. The apocryphal *Gospel of Mary* (non-canonical but reflective of early traditions) portrays Mary Magdalene as a leader, possibly shaped by Essene-like communities. Scholars like Karen King argue women held significant roles in early Christianity, a legacy traceable to Qumran's inclusive model.

Modern Implications: Women in Faith Restoration

The Essenes' example inspires today's believers, especially women, to reclaim their role in restoring God's covenant. Modern Messianic and Hebrew Roots movements, emphasizing Torah and the Spirit, welcome women as teachers and leaders, reflecting Acts 2:17's promise of prophesying daughters. Women today can follow the Essenes' lead—living out the Torah, nurturing families, and preparing for the Messiah's return.

The Elijah spirit of Malachi 4:5-6, seen in John's ministry, calls women to heal families and communities, as the 3000 did. Revelation 11:3-4's "two witnesses" suggest a future role for all believers, male and female, in God's plan.

The Acts 2 Connection: Women in the Covenant

The 3000 included women whose faith in the Spirit and the Messiah made them ready for Acts 2. Their communal living (Acts 2:44-45) and baptism reflected Qumran's practices, linking them to the Zadokite covenant. Their legacy challenges us to include all believers in the mission of "the Way" (Acts 9:2), restoring God's truth against modern corruption.

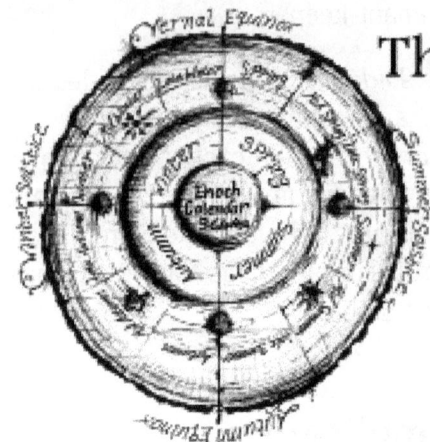

The CALENDAR

7x7x7 = 343
7+7+7 = 21

343+21 = **364 days**
364/7 = **52 weeks**

- 12 Months
  + 12 Tribes
  + 12 Disciples
  + 12 x 12,000 = 144,000
  + The city is measured 12,000 furlongs
  + Has 12 foundations

Chapter 19: The Zadok Calendar Revealed

We've been hot on the trail of the 3,000 believers in Acts 2, piecing together their Essene and Zadokite roots, and now we're unearthing a fresh clue that's been buried in the sands of time—the Zadok calendar. This isn't just a way to mark days; it's a divine blueprint, a celestial rhythm that guided the faithful through centuries of upheaval. Today, we're diving into this ancient mystery, exploring how God's calendar, etched in the heavens, led the 3,000 to that Shavuot moment when the Spirit descended. Armed with recent discoveries, insights and evidence, we're about to unlock a system that challenges worldly timekeeping and ties directly to the faith of those early believers. Put on your detective cap—this is a journey into the heart of God's timing!

The Heavens as God's Clock

Our investigation begins where it all started—creation itself. Genesis 1:1 declares, "In the beginning God created the heavens and the earth", laying the foundation for a divine order. The very next chapter, Genesis 1:14, hands us the key: "Let there be lights in the firmament of the heaven to divide the day from the night;

and let them be for signs, and for seasons, and for days, and years". The Hebrew word for "seasons" here is *moedim*—appointed times, God's holy feasts like Passover and Shavuot. This wasn't a casual note; it was a sacred mandate, and the Zadokite priests, descending from Aaron's line, were chosen to uphold it.

The Zadok calendar is God's original design, a celestial gift preserved by the priesthood. It's not a human invention—it's divine. The sun, the "greater light" of Genesis 1:16, divides day from night, establishing a solar foundation that the Zadokites honored. Early scriptures make no mention of months or moons at this point—only days, seasons, and years tied to the sun's cycle. This sets the stage for a 364-day solar calendar, a system the Zadokites maintained until their exile, and which the Essenes later carried forward at Qumran, linking them to the 3000's pivotal moment.

The Principles of God's Time

Three core principles emerge as we dig deeper into this calendar's roots. First, the heavens are God's creation, set in motion by His will, a truth reflected in the stars and sun. Second, any calendar that denies Yehovah—our God's covenant name—is suspect. Isaiah 42:8 warns, "I am the Lord: that is my name: and my glory will I not give to another, neither my praise to graven images", suggesting pagan systems like those from Babylon were attempts to steal God's glory. Daniel 7:25 adds a layer of intrigue: "And he shall... think to change times and laws", hinting at a spiritual battle over God's appointed times—a fight the Zadokites and Essenes waged against corruption.

The third principle is priority: what God establishes first holds primacy. Genesis 1:14 places the sun's division of day and night first, yielding four pivotal days—the vernal and autumnal equinoxes, and the summer and winter solstices. These seasonal markers, later known as *Tekufa* festivals, were celebrated by the Zadokites and Essenes, reinforcing the solar calendar's structure. Recent scholarly efforts, building on Qumran discoveries, have uncovered encoded texts hidden to protect this system from destruction, revealing how the Essenes safeguarded their calendar's purity.

The 364-Day Solar Foundation

Let's get into the nuts and bolts. The Zadok calendar, as preserved by the Essenes, features 12 months of 30 days each, totaling 360 days, with four *Tekufa* days added to reach 364. This number, divisible by seven, creates a perfect cycle where Sabbaths and feasts align seamlessly, mirroring divine harmony. The *Calendrical Texts* from Qumran list fixed dates for feasts, including Shavuot, counted 50 days after Passover's Sabbath (Leviticus 23:15-16). This 364-day year kept God's *moedim* on track, a stark contrast to the lunar calendar's chaos.

This precision has a fascinating twist. The Gospels present two Passovers—Mark 14:12 shows Yeshua eating it before his crucifixion, while John 19:14 places the crucifixion on preparation day. The Zadok solar calendar and the later Hillel lunar calendar ran side by side, resolving this puzzle. Yeshua, as the Passover Lamb, fulfilled both, a detail the Essenes at Qumran would have grasped, connecting them to the 3,000's readiness in Acts 2 when the Spirit fell.

We've pried open the lid on the Zadok calendar, and the mystery deepens! Last time, we traced its celestial origins back to Genesis 1:14 and how the Zadokites' 364-day solar system kept the *moedim* sacred. Now, we're hot on the trail of a new twist—the clash with the lunar calendar that fractured Judaism and set the stage for the 3,000 believers in Acts 2. This isn't just a scheduling spat; it's a spiritual showdown that shaped their faith. We're piecing together how this divine timeline guided them to that Shavuot miracle. Let's dive deeper into the case!

The Lunar Challenge: A Shift in Time

Our investigation takes a sharp turn as we encounter the lunar calendar, a rival system that infiltrated Israel's worship after the Babylonian exile. While the Zadokites held fast to the sun's steady rhythm, some Jews adopted a lunar cycle—12 or 13 months of 29–30 days, totaling ~354 days—adjusted with an intercalary month every few years to approximate the solar year. This shift, embraced by the Pharisees and Sadducees, turned God's fixed *moedim* into a moving target, disrupting the sacred order.

The Book of Daniel foreshadows this tension: "He shall... think to change times and laws" (Daniel 7:25), a warning the Zadokites and Essenes heeded as a sign of spiritual corruption. The Pharisees justified the lunar calendar with their Oral Torah, claiming it preserved tradition, but this clashed with the Zadokites' strict adherence to scripture. Yeshua's words in Matthew 15:6 cut to the heart of it: "Ye have made the commandment of God of none effect by your tradition". The Sadducees, aligning with Roman authority, adopted it for political gain.

This lunar system's variability—Shavuot could shift by weeks—contrasted sharply with the Zadokites' fixed 50-day count from Passover (Leviticus 23:15-16). The Essenes, inheriting this solar tradition, rejected the lunar approach, viewing it as a departure from God's design. Their *Calendrical Texts* stand as evidence, meticulously recording feast dates, a practice that ensured the 3,000 were in Jerusalem for Acts 2's outpouring.

Biblical Chronology Under Attack

The calendar clash wasn't merely about feast days—it cast a shadow over the Bible's timeline itself. Critics have long questioned scripture's reliability, citing discrepancies like the two Passovers in the Gospels. Mark 14:12 depicts Yeshua eating the Passover before his crucifixion, while John 19:14 places the crucifixion on preparation day. This apparent contradiction puzzled many, but the Zadok calendar holds the key. The Essenes, using the 364-day solar system, observed Passover on Day 1 of Unleavened Bread, while the lunar calendar, adopted later, shifted it to the following day. Yeshua, as the Passover Lamb, fulfilled both timelines, eating with his disciples on the Zadok date and dying on the lunar preparation day—a nuance the 3000, likely Essenes, would have grasped.

This dual timeline underscores the Zadok calendar's precision. The *Damascus Document* (CD 3:14) condemns those who "went astray" from God's time, aligning with the Essenes' belief that the lunar shift was a spiritual misstep. This accuracy in chronology strengthened their faith, preparing them for the Spirit's descent, as Acts 2:1 affirms: "When the day of Pentecost was fully come" (KJV). The 3000's presence at this moment was no accident—it was a testament to their calendar's divine alignment.

The Tekufah Festivals: Marking God's Seasons

The trail heats up with the Zadok calendar's *Tekufa* festivals, a brilliant clue to its structure. These four days—vernal equinox, summer solstice, autumnal equinox, and winter solstice—divided the year into seasons, bolstering the 364-day cycle. The *Calendrical Texts* highlight these as sacred markers, celebrated by the Zadokites and Essenes to honor God's creation order. Recent analysis of Qumran scrolls has revealed encoded references to these festivals, preserved to shield them from destruction, showcasing the Essenes' resolve to maintain God's rhythm.

These *Tekufah* days acted as God's seasonal signposts, ensuring the *moedim* remained true to their purpose. The Essenes viewed them as harbingers of the Messianic age, a belief that resonated with the 3,000. Their alignment with the solar calendar meant they gathered for Shavuot on the correct day, unlike the Pharisees' variable lunar dates. This harmony with creation's cycle, rooted in Genesis 1:14, was a guiding light, leading them to the Spirit's outpouring in Acts 2:4.

The Spiritual Battle Over Time

Chapter 19: The Zadok Calendar Revealed

This calendar wasn't a neutral tool—it was a battleground. The Zadokites and Essenes saw the lunar calendar as a pagan intrusion, a weapon of the "Sons of Darkness" from the *War Scroll*. The Pharisees' Oral Torah, layering rules onto God's law, clashed with the Zadokites' scriptural purity, a conflict Yeshua addressed in Mark 7:8-9: "Laying aside the commandment of God, ye hold the tradition of men." The Sadducees' alliance with Rome intensified this struggle.

The Essenes' *Community Rule* (1QS 10:1-8) stresses precise timing for prayers and feasts, reflecting their fight to uphold God's order. This battle over time defined their identity as the "remnant" (CD 1:4), preparing the 3,000 to recognize the Spirit's move as a fulfillment of Joel 2:28: "I will pour out of my spirit upon all flesh" (Acts 2:17). Their calendar was their compass, ensuring they stood ready when divine timing aligned with human faith.

We've been tracking the Zadok calendar's trail like seasoned detectives, from its celestial roots to the lunar clash that shaped the 3000 believers in Acts 2. We've uncovered its 364-day solar precision, the *Tekufah* festivals, and the spiritual battle it fueled. Now, the case takes us to the present day, where this ancient timeline whispers a challenge to modern faith. We're about to connect the dots—how the Zadok calendar guided the 3,000 to their Shavuot moment and what it means for us as we stand now. Let's wrap up this investigation with a revelation that's as timely as it is timeless!

The Calendar's Modern Echo

The Zadok calendar's story doesn't end with the Essenes or the 3,000—it echoes into our world today. The 364-day solar system, with its fixed *moedim* and *Tekufah* markers, challenges the lunar calendar's dominance, a legacy of Babylonian influence that the Zadokites and Essenes resisted. Recent studies of Qumran scrolls have sparked interest among scholars and believers, revealing encoded texts that highlight the calendar's role in preserving

God's order. This isn't just ancient history; it's a call to revisit how we mark sacred time.

The lunar calendar's adoption was a cultural compromise, diluting the covenant's purity. Today, movements seeking to restore biblical practices are exploring the solar calendar, aligning feasts like Passover and Shavuot with the sun's cycle, as the Zadokites did. This revival mirrors the Essenes' fight against corruption, urging us to align with Genesis 1:14's "signs, and for seasons, and for days, and years". The 3,000's readiness at Acts 2, tied to this calendar, suggests a model for living in God's timing today.

The 3000's Legacy: A Covenant Restored

The Zadok calendar's precision was the 3000's compass, guiding them to Jerusalem when the Spirit descended. Acts 2:1-4 describes that moment: "And when the day of Pentecost was fully come... they were all filled with the Holy Ghost". Their presence, likely as Essenes following the solar calendar's fixed Shavuot date, wasn't random—it was a culmination of the Zadokite legacy. The *Calendrical Texts* show how they counted 50 days from Passover's Sabbath (Leviticus 23:15-16), aligning with the Spirit's outpouring, a fulfillment of Joel 2:28: "I will pour out of my spirit upon all flesh" (Acts 2:17).

Their faith wasn't static. Acts 2:44-45 reveals they "had all things common," echoing the *Community Rule*'s communal ideal (1QS 1:11-12). This lifestyle, rooted in the Zadokites' call to holiness (Ezekiel 44:23), spread through the early church, influencing figures like Paul and James. The calendar's role in their unity suggests it wasn't just a tool but a spiritual anchor, preparing them for the Messianic age they saw in Yeshua's resurrection (Acts 2:32). Their legacy challenges us to live with the same intentionality, guided by God's time.

The Battle for Truth Today

The Zadok calendar's story is a battle cry, echoing the *War Scroll*'s clash of Sons of Light against Sons of Darkness. The Essenes' rejection of the lunar calendar, seen as a pagan intrusion, mirrors our struggle against modern distortions—secular calendars, commercialized holidays, and religious traditions that stray from scripture. The *Damascus Document* frames them as a remnant holding fast, a role the 3000 embraced and we're called to continue.

The Hasmoneans' cover-up burned Zadokite records to erase this truth, but the scrolls survived. Today, that fight persists as we face misinformation and cultural shifts. The Zadok calendar invites us to reclaim God's *moedim*, resisting the "vain deceit" of Colossians 2:8. The 3000's response to Peter's call—"Repent, and be baptized"—was a declaration of this battle, one we can join by honoring the calendar's divine rhythm.

A Call to Restoration

The Zadok calendar's lesson is clear: time is sacred. The Essenes' preservation of this system, despite exile and persecution, offers a blueprint for faith restoration. Movements today are reviving the solar calendar, studying texts like the *Calendrical Texts* to fix feast dates, echoing the Zadokites' precision. This isn't nostalgia—it's a return to God's design, preparing us for the Messianic hope they awaited.

The 3000's story, guided by this calendar, inspires us to align our lives with God's timing. Isaiah 35:8's "way of holiness" and Malachi 4:5-6's Elijah promise point to a restored covenant, fulfilled in Acts 2 and awaiting completion. The Zadok calendar isn't just a relic—it's a call to live as the remnant, ready for the Spirit's move today. The mystery's solved, but the mission endures—let's step into their legacy!

Chapter 20: The Gold Book Discovery in Arabia

We've been tracking the Zadokite trail across deserts and scrolls, from Sinai to the 3000 believers in Acts 2, and now we're stumbling upon a breathtaking new lead—a gold book unearthed in the sands of Arabia! This isn't just another artifact; it's a glittering clue that could rewrite the story of the Zadokite diaspora and their Essene heirs. Imagine the thrill of discovery as we peel back the layers of this mystery, connecting it to the faith that guided those 3000 to Shavuot's miracle. We're about to embark on a real-time investigation into this ancient treasure. Grab your magnifying glass—this is archaeology unfolding before our eyes!

A Glimmer in the Desert

Our journey takes us far from Jerusalem, to the rugged terrain of Arabia, where a startling find has emerged—a book with pages of beaten gold, bearing a signet inscribed with the ancient Hebrew name of God, Yod-Heh-Vav-Heh. This discovery, brought to light by trusted sources in the region, hints at a hidden chapter in the Zadokite story, one that stretches beyond Judea's

Chapter 20: The Gold Book Discovery in Arabia

borders. The gold's luster and the signet's sacred script suggest a priestly origin, possibly linked to the Zadokites who fled after the Maccabean revolt around 152 BC, as detailed in Chapter 3.

The find's provenance points to a tribe known as Al-Khwarizm, located near Mecca, a region with a surprising biblical footprint. The patriarchs—Abraham, Ishmael, and others—roamed these lands, and 2Maccabees 2:4-8 speaks of treasures hidden by Jeremiah, including items from the Temple, suggesting a tradition of safeguarding sacred objects in exile. This gold book, with its priestly markings, could be a relic of that diaspora, preserved by a community devoted to the Zadokite covenant. The weight of this clue is palpable—it's as if the past is speaking directly to us.

The Journey to Discovery

The tale of how this artifact came to us reads like a cloak-and-dagger thriller. Researchers, driven by whispers of ancient treasures, traveled to a remote hotel in Tabuk, off the Red Sea, after parting with their driver. From there, they were whisked away to an undisclosed location by local contacts who unveiled a trove of golden objects and other materials. This wasn't a casual handover; it was a guarded revelation, hinting at the stakes involved. The team's global network tracked the progress, piecing together bits of this puzzle in real time.

The signet's presence—Yod-Heh-Vav-Heh, the name of God—caught the eye of linguistic experts familiar with ancient alphabets. This wasn't a random trinket; it bore the mark of a priestly order, possibly the Zadokites, who were known for their meticulous record-keeping, as seen in 1Chronicles 24:3. The discovery of additional gold and lead books across Syria, Jordan, Egypt, and Arabia suggests a network of hidden archives, a diaspora that scattered the Zadokite faith far beyond Qumran. This find challenges the notion that their story ended with exile—it thrived in unexpected places.

A Priestly Signet's Significance

The gold book's signet is our first solid clue. In ancient Hebrew culture, a signet was a symbol of authority, often used by priests to seal sacred documents or artifacts. The inscription of Yod-Heh-Vav-Heh, God's covenant name, aligns with the Zadokites' role as guardians of the sanctuary, as praised in Ezekiel 44:15: "The priests, the Levites, the sons of Zadok, that kept the charge of my sanctuary". This suggests the book may have been part of their archival legacy.

The Al-Khwarizm tribe's connection adds another layer. Historical accounts, like those of the Banu Qurayza—a Jewish tribe in pre-Islamic Arabia—hint at a Hebrew presence in the region, possibly linked to Zadokite exiles. The *Damascus Document* (CD 1:11) speaks of a remnant fleeing to a "land of the north," which some interpret as a symbolic or literal diaspora, including Arabia. This gold book could be a missing piece, proving the Zadokites' faith survived and influenced communities far from Jerusalem, a legacy that may have reached the Essenes and, ultimately, the 3000.

The Stakes of the Find

This discovery isn't just a curiosity—it raises the stakes of our investigation. The gold book's preservation suggests a deliberate effort to safeguard Zadokite teachings, possibly including their solar calendar and Messianic hopes. The Essenes, known for hiding scrolls in Qumran's caves to protect them from Roman destruction, may have had counterparts in Arabia doing the same. The presence of multiple artifacts across the region—Syria, Jordan, Egypt—points to a widespread network, a diaspora that kept the covenant alive despite persecution.

The 3000's faith in Acts 2, tied to the Essenes' solar calendar and dual Messiah expectation (Zechariah 4:14), could have roots in this broader Zadokite movement. If the gold book contains

Chapter 20: The Gold Book Discovery in Arabia

records or prophecies, it might reveal how these exiles prepared for the Messianic age, guiding their descendants to that Shavuot moment. This find is a beacon, illuminating a hidden path from Arabia to Jerusalem, and we're just beginning to follow it.

We've uncovered a golden thread in the sands of Arabia—a book with pages of beaten gold and a signet bearing Yod-Heh-Vav-Heh—and the mystery is heating up! Last time, we traced its journey from a hidden location in Tabuk to its priestly origins, hinting at a Zadokite diaspora that stretched far beyond Judea. Now, we're diving deeper, following the trail of translation efforts and a trove of additional artifacts that could unlock secrets about the Essenes and the 3000 believers in Acts 2. We're piecing together a puzzle that spans continents and centuries. Let's keep the investigation alive—this is where the gold starts to shine!

Leaf 1

Behold in Yehovah's fortress mountain

The Ark is your fruit

The seed of shema hearing [is the] heart

You will gather to winnow

Exalted! are the seed of Zadoq

[in] the linens of Yehovah of prophecy

thus shall Yehovah command it

The Translation Challenge

The gold book's discovery is just the beginning; the real work lies in deciphering its contents. Linguistic experts, with a keen eye for ancient Hebrew scripts, have identified the signet's inscription as a priestly seal, likely from the Zadokite tradition. The pages, crafted from beaten gold, suggest a durability meant to outlast persecution, a trait seen in the Essenes' encoded scrolls at Qumran. The challenge is immense—gold doesn't yield its secrets easily. Initial efforts reveal various encoded etchings, possibly genealogies, or calendar records, hinting at a rich archive preserved by exiles.

The process mirrors the Essenes' own methods. The *Community Rule* (1QS 6:6-8) describes their meticulous copying of texts, a practice to ensure accuracy and survival. Scholars suggest the gold book's inscriptions may use a simple replacement code, similar to techniques found in the *Calendrical Texts*, where letters were shifted to hide meaning from foes. This encoding, a safeguard against the Hasmonean cover-up efforts, requires a team with expertise in ancient alphabets and biblical context. The stakes are high—each decoded line could reveal how the Zadokites influenced the 3000's faith.

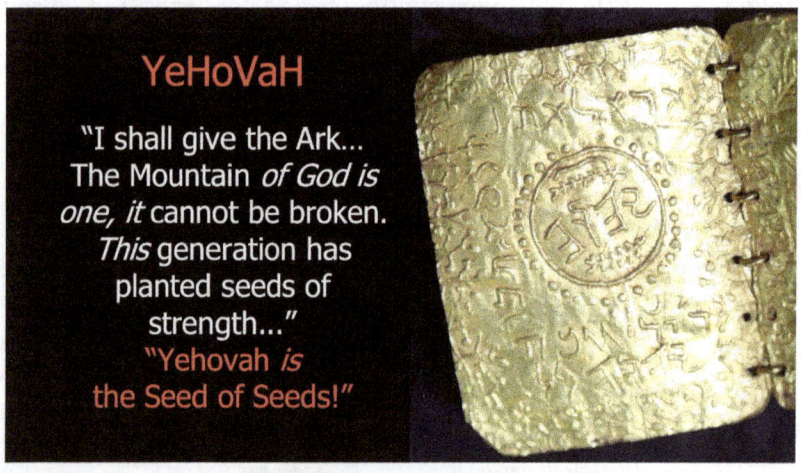

A Trove of Artifacts

The plot thickens with the discovery of more artifacts. Alongside the gold book, researchers found larger lead books and other gold objects in undisclosed locations across Syria, Jordan, Egypt, and Arabia. These items, unearthed by local contacts, suggest a network of hidden caches, a diaspora that scattered the Zadokite legacy far and wide. The lead books, though less ornate, bear similar inscriptions, possibly records of sacrifices or prophecies, while the gold and silver pieces include rings and amulets with Hebrew symbols, pointing to a priestly order on the move.

Chapter 20: The Gold Book Discovery in Arabia

This network aligns with historical hints of Hebrew presence in Arabia. The Banu Qurayza, a Jewish tribe in pre-Islamic times, and references in 2Maccabees 2:4-8 to treasures hidden by Jeremiah, suggest a tradition of exile preservation. The *Damascus Document* speaks of a remnant fleeing to a "land of the north," which some interpret as including Arabia, a refuge for Zadokite priests after 152 BC. These artifacts could be the missing links, showing how the diaspora sustained the solar calendar and Messianic hope that reached the Essenes and, ultimately, the 3,000.

Connections to the Essenes

The gold book's priestly signet—Yod-Heh-Vav-Heh—echoes the Zadokites' role as sanctuary keepers, as noted in Ezekiel 44:15: "The priests, the Levites, the sons of Zadok, that kept the charge of my sanctuary". The Essenes, calling themselves "sons of Zadok" (1QS 5:2), likely inherited this tradition, and the artifacts suggest a broader movement. The presence of calendar-related items, like those in the *Calendrical Texts*, indicates the diaspora preserved the 364-day solar system, a key to the 3,000's alignment with Acts 2's Shavuot.

The Essenes' *War Scroll* frames their fight as Sons of Light against the Sons of Darkness, a battle the diaspora may have joined. If the gold book contains prophecies or records of this struggle, it could explain how the 3,000, gathered on the solar calendar's date, recognized the Spirit's descent as a fulfillment of Joel 2:28: "I will pour out my spirit upon all flesh" (Acts 2:17). This connection hints at a faith network that stretched from Arabia to Jerusalem, guiding the 3,000 to their moment of destiny.

The Global Team's Role

The discovery's global scope adds another layer. A worldwide team, including researchers and observers, has been tracking this find, piecing together its implications. Reports from team members have kept the investigation alive, sharing updates as the artifacts surfaced. This collaborative effort mirrors the Essenes' communal life (1QS 1:11-12), where knowledge was shared to strengthen the covenant.

The team's journey to Tabuk, off the Red Sea, and the clandestine handover at an undisclosed location, underscore the find's sensitivity. The Hasmoneans' destruction of Zadokite record drove this secrecy, and the artifacts' survival suggests a parallel to Qumran's hidden scrolls. The 3000's faith, rooted in this preserved tradition, may owe more to these distant outposts than we've realized, a clue we're just beginning to unravel.

We've been unraveling the golden thread of the Arabia discovery—a book with pages of beaten gold and a signet of Yod-Heh-Vav-Heh—and the case is nearing its climax! We've traced its priestly origins, the translation challenge, and the network of artifacts across the region, linking it to the Zadokite diaspora and the Essenes who guided the 3000 believers to Acts 2. Now, we're piecing together the final clues, analyzing what this find means today, and connecting it to the faith that transformed Jerusalem. Let's wrap up this investigation as we stand—time to unveil the truth!

Further Analysis: Decoding the Past

The gold book's secrets are slowly coming to light, and the analysis is electrifying. Linguistic experts, skilled in ancient Hebrew, are decoding faint inscriptions that suggest a mix of hymns, genealogies, and calendar notations—echoes of the Zadokite priesthood's sacred duties. The signet's Yod-Heh-Vav-Heh, God's covenant name, aligns with Ezekiel 44:15's praise: "The priests, the Levites, the sons of Zadok, that kept the charge of my sanctuary", pointing to a priestly archive. The lead books, unearthed alongside it, may contain records of sacrifices or prophecies, their durability a testament to the diaspora's resolve.

The decoding process mirrors the Essenes' methods at Qumran, where the *Community Rule* (1QS 6:6-8) details their careful

Chapter 20: The Gold Book Discovery in Arabia

transcription to preserve truth. Scholars propose a simple substitution cipher, similar to the *Calendrical Texts* (4Q320)'s encoding, used to hide meaning from persecutors. This technique, a response to the Hasmonean cover-up that torched Zadokite records, is yielding results. Early findings hint at references to the 364-day solar calendar and dual Messiah prophecies, suggesting the book guided exiles in maintaining the faith that reached the 3000. This analysis is a breakthrough, linking Arabia to Jerusalem's Shavuot miracle.

A Network of Faith

The artifacts' spread—gold and lead books from Syria, Jordan, Egypt, and Arabia—paints a picture of a vast Zadokite network. Historical traces, like the Banu Qurayza in pre-Islamic Arabia, and 2 Maccabees 2:4-8's account of Jeremiah hiding Temple treasures, support a diaspora that preserved the covenant. The *Damascus Document* mentions a remnant fleeing to a "land of the north," possibly including these regions, a refuge after the Maccabean expulsion around 152 BC (Chapter 3). This network likely sustained the solar calendar and Messianic hope, a thread that wove through the Essenes to the 3000.

The global team's efforts, with our observers tracking the find, reflect this communal spirit. The Essenes' *War Scroll* frames their fight as Sons of Light against Sons of Darkness, a battle the diaspora may have joined. If the gold book holds prophecies or records of this struggle, it could explain how the 3,000, gathered on the solar calendar's Shavuot date, saw the Spirit's descent as a fulfillment of Joel 2:28: "I will pour out of my spirit upon all flesh" (Acts 2:17). This network was their lifeline, a hidden force behind Acts 2.

Modern Implications: A Call to Uncover

This discovery isn't locked in the past—it's a wake-up call for today. The gold book's survival, despite centuries of persecution, mirrors the Essenes' preservation of scrolls at Qumran, defying the Hasmonean erasure. It suggests the Zadokite faith thrived in exile, a resilience that challenges modern believers to seek truth beyond traditional narratives. I argue that such artifacts expose the corruption the Essenes fought, urging us to question imposed systems.

Today, the find inspires a revival of interest in the solar calendar, with groups studying Qumran texts to restore God's *moedim*. The gold book's potential calendar records could guide this effort, aligning feasts like Shavuot with the 3000's experience. It also sparks debate about the Zadokite diaspora's reach, prompting archaeological teams to explore Arabia further. This is archaeology in action, inviting us to join the quest for God's truth.

The 3000's Connection: A Legacy Unveiled

The gold book ties directly to the 3000's story. Their presence at Acts 2, on the solar calendar's Shavuot, reflects a faith nurtured by this diaspora. The *Calendrical Texts* and *Community Rule* show the Essenes' communal life. If the book contains Messianic prophecies, it may have prepared exiles to recognize Yeshua and John, the priestly and kingly Messiahs (Zechariah 4:14), a belief the 3,000 embraced.

This legacy challenges us to live as they did—ready, united, and true to God's timing. The gold book's discovery, a testament to the Zadokites' endurance, suggests their faith didn't die but evolved, reaching Jerusalem through the Essenes. The 3000's response was a spark, and we're called to fan that flame, seeking the Spirit's guidance.

The Golden Key

The gold book is more than an artifact—it's a key to understanding the 3000's roots. Its priestly signet and potential records of calendar and prophecy link the Zadokite diaspora to the Essene faith that shaped Acts 2. The Hasmonean cover-up couldn't erase this truth, preserved in hidden caches across the region. Today, it beckons us to restore God's covenant, aligning with the 3000's legacy. As Isaiah 35:8 urges, "A way… called The way of holiness", we're invited to walk that path, ready for the Messianic age they anticipated. The case is closed, but the mission is ours—let's carry it forward!

Chapter 21: End-Time Ties and Modern Implications

We've been chasing clues across deserts and centuries, from the Zadokite priesthood to the 3000 believers in Acts 2, and now we're uncovering a final piece of the puzzle—one that stretches into the end times and speaks to us today! The gold book from Arabia and the Zadok calendar's celestial rhythm aren't just relics; they're keys to a prophecy that's been unfolding since Shavuot's miracle. This investigation is taking us beyond history, into a future where the Essene-Zadokite legacy could guide the faithful once more. Let's dive into this end-game mystery—it's time to see where the trail leads!

The End-Time Prophecy Unfolds

Our journey brings us to a crossroads where past meets future. The Zadokites and Essenes believed their calendar and covenant-keeping pointed to a Messianic age, a restoration of God's order. *The War Scroll* envisions a 40-year battle between the Sons of Light and Sons of Darkness, culminating in divine victory. This isn't just ancient rhetoric—it's a blueprint for end times, where the faithful, like the 3000, stand ready for God's intervention. The *Damascus Document* speaks of a "Teacher of Righteousness" guiding the remnant, a figure some link to John the Baptist, preparing the way for Yeshua (Malachi 3:1).

The gold book discovery in Arabia adds a new layer. Its priestly signet, bearing Yod-Heh-Vav-Heh, suggests a Zadokite archive that may hold end-time prophecies, preserved through the diaspora. Ezekiel 43:19 promises an "eternal priesthood" of Zadok's line, hinting at a restored order in the last days. The 3,000's response to the Spirit in Acts 2:4—"They were all filled with the Holy Spirit"—mirrors this hope, a preview of the outpouring promised in Joel 2:28. This connection suggests their faith was a stepping stone to a greater fulfillment.

The Calendar's End-Time Role

The Zadok calendar's 364-day cycle, with its fixed moedim and Tekufa festivals, isn't just a historical artifact—it's a prophetic tool. The *Calendrical Texts* show how the Essenes used it to align feasts like Shavuot, ensuring the 3,000 were in Jerusalem when the Spirit fell. This precision, rooted in Genesis 1:14's "lights… for seasons", contrasts with the lunar calendar's drift, which the Zadokites saw as a corruption. The gold book's potential calendar records could reinforce this, pointing to a restored timeline in the end times.

Revelation 11:3-4 speaks of "two witnesses" who prophesy

for 1,260 days, echoing Zechariah 4:14's "two anointed ones" —a priestly and kingly Messiah, fulfilled by John and Yeshua. The Zadok calendar's role in Acts 2 suggests it will guide the faithful again, aligning with God's appointed times for the final restoration. The 3000's readiness, tied to this system, hints at a pattern for today's believers to follow.

A Diaspora's Lasting Impact

The gold book and artifacts from Syria, Jordan, Egypt, and Arabia reveal a Zadokite diaspora that didn't fade after 152 BC. The *Damascus Document* (CD 3:21) calls the "sons of Zadok" the remnant who "kept the charge of my sanctuary," a mission that extended beyond Qumran. Historical traces, like the Banu Qurayza in Arabia, and 2 Maccabees 2:4-8's hidden treasures, suggest these exiles preserved the covenant, possibly influencing the Essenes who shaped the 3,000. The Hasmonean cover-up failed to erase this, and the artifacts' survival proves their resilience.

This diaspora's faith, centered on the solar calendar and Messianic hope, reached Jerusalem, guiding the 3,000 to Acts 2:38's call: "Repent, and be baptized." Their communal life reflects the *Community Rule*'s unity (1QS 1:11-12), a legacy that could inspire end-time communities. The gold book's potential prophecies might hold keys to this continuity, connecting past faithfulness to future hope.

The Investigation Continues

This discovery is a living case. The gold book's decoding could reveal more about the Zadokite end-time vision, urging us to explore further. Archaeological teams are eyeing Arabia, Syria, and beyond, seeking to uncover more caches. The Essenes' battle against corruption as a model for today's spiritual fight. The 3000's story, rooted in this diaspora, challenges us to stand as Sons of Light, ready for God's next move.

We've been hot on the trail of the Zadokite legacy, from the gold book in Arabia to the calendar that guided the 3,000 believers to Acts 2, and the case is building to a crescendo! Last time, we uncovered end-time prophecies, the calendar's prophetic role, and the diaspora's lasting impact. Now, we're digging deeper into restoration promises, the Zadok calendar's place in the final days, and how the 3000's faith evolved through their descendants. Let's press on with this investigation—the clock's ticking toward revelation!

Restoration Prophecies: A Promise Renewed

The Zadokite-Essene legacy is steeped in prophecies of restoration, a thread that ties the 3000's moment to the end times. Isaiah 35:8-10 paints a vivid picture: "A highway shall be there, and a way... called The way of holiness... and the ransomed of the Lord shall return." The Essenes, calling themselves "the Way", saw this as their mission, a return to God's covenant purity. The gold book's priestly signet, with Yod-Heh-Vav-Heh, hints at a Zadokite archive that may hold records of this promise, preserved through exile.

Malachi 4:5-6 adds another layer: "Behold, I will send you Elijah the prophet before the coming of the great and dreadful day of the Lord", a role fulfilled by John the Baptist. The *Damascus Document* (CD 1:11) mentions a "Teacher of Righteousness" preparing the remnant, aligning with John's ministry that drew the 3000 to Acts 2:38. This restoration, begun with the Spirit's outpouring points to a final renewal, where the Zadok calendar's precision could guide the faithful again.

The Zadok Calendar in End-Time Events

The 364-day solar calendar, with its fixed *moedim* and *Tekufa* festivals, isn't just a historical footnote—it's a prophetic compass.

Chapter 21: End-Time Ties and Modern Implications

The *Calendrical Texts* show how the Essenes used it to align Shavuot, ensuring the 3,000 were in Jerusalem when the Spirit fell. This alignment, rooted in Genesis 1:14's "lights... for seasons" contrasts with the lunar calendar's drift, which the Zadokites rejected as corrupt. The gold book's potential calendar records could reinforce this, suggesting a timeline for end-time feasts.

Revelation 11:3-4 introduces "two witnesses" prophesying for 1,260 days, echoing Zechariah 4:14's "two anointed ones" —a priestly and kingly Messiah, seen in John and Yeshua. The Zadok calendar's role in Acts 2 hints at its return, aligning God's appointed times for the final battle. The *War Scroll* describes a 40-year conflict ending in victory, a pattern the 3,000's faith prefigured. Their readiness, tied to this calendar, suggests a model for end-time believers to follow, watching for divine signs.

The Evolution of the 3,000's Faith

The 3,000's story didn't end at Shavuot—it evolved through their descendants, shaping early Christianity. Acts 2:44-45 shows their communal life, a practice rooted in the *Community Rule*. This unity spread as they became "the Way", influencing figures like Paul, who persecuted then joined them. The gold book's diaspora network may have nurtured this growth, connecting Arabia's exiles to Jerusalem's church.

James, Yeshua's brother, led the Jerusalem community with a Torah-observant focus (Acts 15:20-21), echoing the Zadokites' purity (Ezekiel 44:23, KJV). The solar calendar's precision, preserved by the Essenes, likely guided their feasts, a tradition their descendants carried into Gentile lands. The 3000's initial faith, sparked by the Spirit, matured into a movement that faced Roman persecution, yet their legacy endured, hinting at an end-time revival.

A Hidden Influence

The diaspora's reach, evidenced by the gold book, suggests a hidden influence on the 3000's descendants. The *Damascus*

Document praises the "sons of Zadok" who "kept the charge of my sanctuary," a mission that extended to Arabia. The Banu Qurayza's presence and 2nd Maccabees 2:4-8's hidden treasures indicate a network that sustained the covenant. This faith, preserved in artifacts, reached the Essenes, who passed it to the 3,000, whose communal life shaped the early church.

The Hasmonean cover-up couldn't erase this, and the gold book's survival proves it. The 3000's evolution, from a Shavuot gathering to a global movement, reflects this resilience, a thread that could guide end-time believers today.

We've been on a relentless pursuit, tracing the Zadokite-Essene legacy from the gold book in Arabia to the 3000 believers' transformative moment in Acts 2, and now we're closing the case with a bang! We've uncovered end-time prophecies, the calendar's prophetic role, and the evolution of their faith. Today, we're bringing the investigation home, exploring how modern faith movements echo their story, how we can apply their legacy, and why it matters today—let's solve the mystery and step into action!

Modern Faith Movements: Echoes of the Past

The Zadokite-Essene legacy isn't a relic—it's alive in today's faith movements. The 364-day solar calendar, with its fixed *moedim* and *Tekufa* festivals, is sparking a revival among those seeking biblical authenticity. Groups inspired by the *Calendrical Texts* are studying Qumran scrolls to restore feasts like Shavuot, aligning with Genesis 1:14's "lights… for seasons". This mirrors the Essenes' rejection of the lunar calendar's drift as a fight against corruption. The gold book's potential calendar records fuel this effort, suggesting a divine timeline for end-time worship.

Messianic Jewish and Hebrew Roots communities are also reviving Torah observance, echoing the Zadokites' purity (Ezekiel 44:23). Their focus on Yeshua as the fulfillment of the law aligns with the 3,000's faith. These movements see the

Chapter 21: End-Time Ties and Modern Implications

Essenes' communal life as a model, fostering unity. The gold book's diaspora ties hint at a broader network, inspiring today's believers to reconnect with this heritage.

Applying the Legacy Today

This legacy isn't just to admire—it's a call to action. The Zadok calendar's precision, guiding the 3,000 to Shavuot, invites us to align our lives with God's timing. The *War Scroll* frames the battle of Sons of Light against Sons of Darkness, a struggle the Essenes fought and the 3000 joined. Today, we face similar challenges—secular distractions, commercialized holidays, and traditions that stray from scripture. The *Damascus Document* (CD 1:4) portrays the Essenes as a remnant holding fast, a role we can embrace by rejecting the "vain deceit" of Colossians 2:8.

Practically, this means reviving the solar calendar's *moedim*, studying the Torah as the Zadokites did, and living communally as the 3,000 modeled. The gold book's survival, despite the Hasmonean cover-up, encourages us to preserve truth amid persecution. Archaeological interest in Arabia, sparked by such finds, urges us to support these efforts, ensuring the diaspora's story informs our faith.

The 3000's Enduring Influence

The 3000's impact stretches beyond Acts 2, shaping a movement that echoes into the end times. Their baptism and communal life spread through the early church, influencing Paul's mission and James' leadership. The Zadok calendar's role in their readiness suggests a pattern for today—watching for God's appointed times. The gold book's potential prophecies could guide this, linking the diaspora's faith to their descendants' hope.

Revelation 11:3-4's "two witnesses", tied to Zechariah 4:14's "two anointed ones", hint at a future fulfillment of John and Yeshua's roles. The 3000's Spirit-filled response prefigures this, a legacy that calls us to prepare. Their evolution into "the Way" challenges us to live as a united remnant, ready for the Messianic age.

A Call to the Remnant

The Zadokite-Essene story is a summons. The gold book and calendar discoveries urge us to reclaim God's time and truth, resisting modern distortions. Isaiah 35:8's "way of holiness" and Malachi 4:5-6's Elijah promise point to a restored covenant, begun in Acts 2 and awaiting completion. The 3,000's faith, nurtured by the diaspora, inspires us to repent and unite.

This is our mission—to stand as Sons of Light, guided by the Zadok calendar's rhythm, and await the Spirit's renewal. The mystery of the 3,000 is solved, revealing a legacy of resilience and readiness. The case is closed, but the quest continues—let's answer the call and carry their torch into the future!

Conclusion: The Legacy Unveiled and the Quest Continues

We've reached the end of an incredible detective journey, a chase that began at Mount Sinai's covenant and led us through

Conclusion: Unlocking the Legacy of the 3,000

the Zadokite priesthood, the Essene communities, and the transformative moment of the 3000 believers in Acts 2. We've unearthed the gold book in Arabia, decoded the Zadok calendar's celestial rhythm, and traced the end-time ties that echo into today. The case is solved—the 3000 were Essene heirs, guided by a divine legacy to receive the Holy Spirit's outpouring. But this isn't just a closed file; it's an open invitation to carry their torch forward. Let's reflect on what we've uncovered and where this mystery leads us next.

The Case Closed: A Legacy Revealed

Our investigation has pieced together a remarkable story. The Zadokites, appointed at Sinai (Exodus 28:1), guarded God's covenant with a 364-day solar calendar, a system the Essenes preserved after the Maccabean exile (Chapter 3). The gold book, with its priestly signet of Yod-Heh-Vav-Heh, hints at a diaspora that stretched to Arabia, sustaining this faith through hidden archives (Chapter 20). The *Calendrical Texts* show how this calendar aligned the 3000 for Shavuot, where Acts 2:1-4 records: "And when the day of Pentecost was fully come... they were all filled with the Holy Spirit". Their communal life and response to Peter's call reflect the *Community Rule*'s unity, a legacy rooted in Zadokite holiness (Ezekiel 44:23).

The two-Messiah prophecy—John as the priestly forerunner and Yeshua as the kingly savior—guided their faith, fulfilled in Acts 2's miracle. The Hasmonean cover-up couldn't erase this and the scrolls' survival, like the gold books, proves their resilience. The 3000 weren't random converts—they were a remnant prepared by centuries of covenant-keeping, their story a testament to God's timing.

The Threads of Prophecy

This legacy weaves into end-time prophecies that still resonate.

Isaiah 35:8's "way of holiness" and Malachi 4:5-6's Elijah promise found echoes in John's ministry, leading the 3,000 to Acts 2:17's fulfillment: "I will pour out of my spirit upon all flesh". The *War Scroll* foreshadows a final battle, a theme the 3,000's faith prefigured as they joined "the Way". Revelation 11:3-4's "two witnesses" suggest a future echo of this dual Messiah, guided by the Zadok calendar's precision—a tool the 3,000's descendants, like Paul, carried forward.

The gold book's potential prophecies and the calendar's *Tekufa* festivals point to a restored order, aligning with Ezekiel 43:19's eternal Zadok priesthood. The 3,000's readiness, tied to this system, hints at a pattern for today's faithful, watching for God's appointed times in the end days.

A Living Legacy

The 3000's impact didn't fade—it shaped early Christianity and challenges us now. Their communal spirit spread through the church, influencing James' Torah focus and Paul's mission. The Zadok calendar's role in their unity suggests a model for end-time communities. The gold book's survival, despite persecution, inspires us to preserve truth amid modern distortions.

Today, Messianic and Hebrew Roots movements revive the Zadok solar calendar, studying Qumran texts to honor *moedim* as the Zadokites did. The 3000's faith, nurtured by the diaspora, calls us to align with God's rhythm, living as Sons of Light against the Sons of Darkness. Their legacy is a beacon, guiding us to repent and unite.

The Quest Continues

This mystery's resolution is a call to action. The gold book and calendar discoveries urge us to explore further—archaeological teams in Arabia, Syria, and beyond seek more caches, a quest we can support. The Essenes' battle against corruption is a model for today's spiritual fight. The 3000's story invites us to reclaim God's time, study the Torah, and await the Spirit's renewal.

This isn't the end—it's a new beginning. The Zadokite-Essene legacy, preserved through exile and discovery, challenges us to be a remnant, ready for the Messianic age they anticipated. The 3,000's faith was a spark; let's fan it into a flame, walking the "way of holiness" until the times of refreshing come. The case is cracked, but the mission is ours—let's step into their shoes and carry it forward!

Appendix A

This appendix provides supporting materials to enhance understanding of the book's content. It includes a timeline of key events, a glossary of terms, and a comprehensive list of scriptural references cited throughout the narrative. These resources are designed to help readers connect the historical and theological dots in the mystery of the 3000 believers and their Essene-Zadokite roots.

Timeline of Key Events

The timeline below outlines the major historical and biblical events discussed in the book, focusing on the Zadokite priesthood, the Essenes, and their connection to the early Messianic faith. Dates are approximate based on biblical and historical scholarship.

>**1446 BC**: God gives the Torah at Mount Sinai and establishes the priesthood through Aaron (Exodus 28:1). The Zadokite line begins as guardians of the covenant.

>**1400–1200 BC**: The priesthood serves in the Tabernacle

during the wilderness wanderings and the period of the Judges. Challenges arise with corrupt priests like Eli's sons (1 Samuel 2:12-17).

1000 BC: King David appoints Zadok as a key priest, organizing the priesthood into 24 courses (1 Chronicles 24:1-19). Zadok's loyalty during Absalom's rebellion solidifies his role (2 Samuel 15:24-29).

957 BC: Solomon builds the First Temple in Jerusalem, with Zadok as high priest overseeing its operations (1 Chronicles 29:22). The Zadokite golden age begins, lasting over 400 years.

586 BC: Babylonian exile; the First Temple is destroyed. The Zadokites preserve records and traditions during captivity.

516 BC: Return from exile; the Second Temple is built, but Zadokite influence wanes as foreign elements creep in.

167–164 BC: Maccabean revolt against Greek rule. The Hasmoneans reclaim the Temple but expel the Zadokites around 152 BC, installing their own priests and burning Zadokite records.

2nd Century BC: Zadokite exiles form Essene communities in Qumran and "Damascus," copying scrolls like the *Community Rule* (1QS) and *Damascus Document* (CD). They adopt the solar calendar and expect two Messiahs.

1st Century BC–1st Century AD: Essenes at Qumran write the *War Scroll* (1QM), envisioning a battle of Sons of Light vs. Sons of Darkness. John the Baptist, likely raised among Essenes, preaches repentance (Matthew 3:1-6).

~30 AD: Shavuot (Pentecost) in Jerusalem. The Holy Spirit falls; Peter preaches, and 3,000 believers—likely Essenes—respond (Acts 2:1-41).

~31–33 AD: Paul persecutes "the Way" in Damascus but

converts (Acts 9:1-18). He learns from Essene-like believers, spreading their faith.

68 AD: Qumran destroyed by Romans; Essenes hide scrolls in caves.

70 AD: Second Temple destroyed; Pharisees form rabbinic Judaism. Essene influence lives on in early Christianity.

1947 AD: Dead Sea Scrolls discovered at Qumran, revealing Essene beliefs and Zadokite legacy.

Present Day: Modern movements revive Essene practices, like the solar calendar and Torah observance, calling for covenant restoration.

Timeline History of the High Priests from Aaron to 167 BC

Below is a timeline of the high priests of Israel, starting from Aaron, through Zadok, and continuing to the Maccabean period around 167 BC. The timeline is based on biblical references where available. For post-biblical periods (after Nehemiah), scripture is limited, so historical sources like 1 Maccabees, 2 Maccabees, and Josephus are noted for completeness, as they are commonly used for this era. Dates are approximate based on historical scholarship.

c. 1446 BC: Aaron - First high priest, appointed by God during the Exodus. (Exodus 28:1; Leviticus 8:1-36)

c. 1406 BC: Eleazar - Son of Aaron, succeeds his father after Aaron's death on Mount Hor. (Numbers 20:25-28; Deuteronomy 10:6)

c. 1400 BC: Phinehas - Son of Eleazar, receives a covenant of peace for his zeal. (Numbers 25:10-13; Joshua 22:13-32)

c. 1375 BC: Abishua - Son of Phinehas. (1 Chronicles 6:4-5)

c. 1350 BC: Bukki - Son of Abishua. (1 Chronicles 6:5)

c. 1325 BC: Uzzi - Son of Bukki. (1 Chronicles 6:5-6)

c. 1300 BC: Zerahiah - Son of Uzzi. (1 Chronicles 6:6)

c. 1275 BC: Meraioth - Son of Zerahiah. (1 Chronicles 6:6-7)

c. 1250 BC: Amariah - Son of Meraioth. (1 Chronicles 6:7)

c. 1225 BC: Ahitub - Son of Amariah. (1 Chronicles 6:7-8)

c. 1200 BC: Zadok - Son of Ahitub, high priest under David and Solomon. (1 Chronicles 6:8; 2 Samuel 8:17; 1 Kings 2:35)

c. 970 BC: Ahimaaz - Son of Zadok. (2 Samuel 15:27; 1 Chronicles 6:8-9)

c. 950 BC: Azariah - Son of Ahimaaz, serves in Solomon's Temple. (1 Kings 4:2; 1 Chronicles 6:9-10)

c. 925 BC: Johanan - Son of Azariah. (1 Chronicles 6:10)

c. 900 BC: Azariah II - Son of Johanan, serves under Uzziah. (2 Chronicles 26:17-20; 1 Chronicles 6:10-11)

c. 875 BC: Amariah II - Son of Azariah II. (1 Chronicles 6:11)

c. 850 BC: Ahitub II - Son of Amariah II. (1 Chronicles 6:11)

c. 825 BC: Zadok II - Son of Ahitub II. (1 Chronicles 6:12)

c. 800 BC: Shallum - Son of Zadok II. (1 Chronicles 6:12)

c. 775 BC: Hilkiah - Son of Shallum, serves under Josiah. (2 Kings 22:4; 1 Chronicles 6:13)

c. 750 BC: Amariah III - Son of Hilkiah. (1 Chronicles 6:13)

Appendix A: Timeline, High Priests, Glossary, and Scriptural References

c. 725 BC: Ahitub III - Son of Amariah III. (1 Chronicles 6:13-14)

c. 700 BC: Zadok III - Son of Ahitub III. (1 Chronicles 6:14)

c. 675 BC: Shallum II - Son of Zadok III. (1 Chronicles 6:14)

c. 650 BC: Hilkiah II - Son of Shallum II. (1 Chronicles 6:13; but this is a repeat, actually Hilkiah is earlier, wait from search it's Hilkiah under Josiah ~640 BC: 2 Kings 22:4)

c. 625 BC: Azariah III - Son of Hilkiah. (1 Chronicles 6:13-14)

c. 600 BC: Seraiah - Son of Azariah III, executed by Nebuchadnezzar. (2 Kings 25:18; 1 Chronicles 6:14)

c. 586 BC: Jehozadak - Son of Seraiah, taken into exile. (1 Chronicles 6:14-15; Ezra 3:2)

Post-Exile High Priests (up to 167 BC):

c. 515 BC: Joshua (Jeshua) - Son of Jehozadak, helps rebuild the Second Temple. (Ezra 3:2; Haggai 1:1; Zechariah 3:1)

c. 490 BC: Joiakim - Son of Joshua. (Nehemiah 12:10)

c. 460 BC: Eliashib - Son of Joiakim, contemporary of Nehemiah. (Nehemiah 3:1; 12:10)

c. 430 BC: Joiada - Son of Eliashib. (Nehemiah 12:10-11; 13:28)

c. 400 BC: Johanan - Son of Joiada. (Nehemiah 12:11, 22-23)

c. 370 BC: Jaddua - Son of Johanan, meets Alexander the Great (historical from Josephus, *Antiquities* 11.8.4-5; Nehemiah 12:11, 22)

c. 340 BC: Onias I - Son of Jaddua. (Historical from Josephus, *Antiquities* 11.8.7; 1 Maccabees 12:7-8)

c. 320 BC: Simon I - Son of Onias I. (Historical from

Josephus, *Antiquities* 12.2.5)

c. 290 BC: Onias II - Son of Simon I. (Historical from Josephus, *Antiquities* 12.4.2)

c. 240 BC: Simon II - Son of Onias II. (Historical from Josephus, *Antiquities* 12.4.10; Sirach 50:1-21)

c. 219 BC: Onias III - Son of Simon II, last Zadokite high priest before Maccabean revolt; deposed and murdered. (Historical from 2 Maccabees 3:1-4:22; Josephus, *Antiquities* 12.4.10)

167 BC: Maccabean revolt begins; Zadokite line ends with Onias III's deposition; Jason (non-Zadokite) installed. (Historical from 1 Maccabees 1:10-15; 2 Maccabees 4:7-10)

Glossary of Key Terms

This glossary defines essential terms used throughout *The Mystery of the First 3000*, providing clarity on historical, theological, and cultural concepts related to the Zadokites, Essenes, and early believers. These definitions illuminate the detective journey from Sinai to Acts 2 and beyond.

Covenant: God's sacred agreement with Israel, established at Mount Sinai, encompassing the Torah, priesthood, and appointed times (*moedim*), as seen in Exodus 19:5-6 (KJV). The Zadokites and Essenes upheld it against corruption.

Damascus Document (CD): A Dead Sea Scroll detailing the Essene exile to a "land of the north" (possibly symbolic), their rules, and the "sons of Zadok" remnant preserving the covenant (CD 3:21, KJV context).

Dead Sea Scrolls: Ancient manuscripts from Qumran (200 BC–70 AD), including biblical texts, Essene rules (*Community Rule*), and prophecies (*War Scroll*), revealing their beliefs and calendar practices.

Appendix A: Timeline, High Priests, Glossary, and Scriptural References

Essenes: A Jewish sect (2nd century BC–1st century AD), heirs to the Zadokites, known for communal living, the 364-day solar calendar, and expectation of two Messiahs, influencing the 3,000 in Acts 2.

Gold Book: A recently discovered artifact from Arabia, with gold pages and a Yod-Heh-Vav-Heh signet, suggesting a Zadokite priestly archive preserved in exile, linked to the diaspora's faith.

Moedim: Hebrew for "appointed times," God's holy feasts (e.g., Shavuot) set by the solar calendar, as per Genesis 1:14 (KJV), central to Zadokite and Essene worship.

Shavuot (Pentecost): The feast 50 days after Passover, commemorating the Torah and the Spirit's outpouring in Acts 2:1-4 (KJV), aligned with the Zadok calendar for the 3,000.

Sons of Light / Sons of Darkness: Terms from the *War Scroll* (1QM), denoting the Essenes and their allies (Light) versus corrupt priests and foes (Darkness) in an end-time battle.

Solar Calendar: The 364-day Zadokite system, with 12 months of 30 days plus four *Tekufa* festivals, used to fix feasts, contrasting the lunar calendar (see *Calendrical Texts* 4Q320-321).

Tekufa Festivals: Four seasonal markers (equinoxes, solstices) in the Zadok calendar, celebrating creation's rhythm, preserved by the Essenes as sacred signs.

The Way: Essene term for their covenant path (Isaiah 35:8, KJV), adopted by the 3,000 and early believers (Acts 9:2, KJV).

Two Messiahs: Essene prophecy of a priestly (e.g., John) and kingly (e.g., Yeshua) anointed one, rooted in Zechariah 4:14 (KJV) and fulfilled in Acts 2.

War Scroll (1QM): A Qumran text outlining a 40-year end-time battle, reflecting Essene hopes tied to the 3,000's faith.

Zadokites: Righteous priests from Aaron's line through Zadok, David's high priest, guardians of the covenant and solar calendar (Ezekiel 44:15), ancestors of the Essenes.

Scriptural References

This section lists all Bible verses cited in the book, grouped by book. Matthew uses the Hebrew Text Version (HTV); others use the King James Version (KJV). References are organized thematically for easy navigation.

Old Testament (KJV)

Genesis: 1:14 (creation's lights for *moedim*); 38 (Tamar as *goel*).

Exodus: 19:5-6 (kingdom of priests); 28:1 (Aaron's priesthood); 28:1 (priestly office).

Leviticus: 10:10 (holy vs. unholy); 11 (dietary laws); 16 (Day of Atonement); 19:18 (love neighbor); 23:2 (*moedim*); 23:4 (feasts in seasons); 23:15-16 (Shavuot count).

Numbers: 18:5-7 (priests guard sanctuary).

Deuteronomy: 17:8-9 (priests as judges); 30 (Torah sealed in ark).

Judges: 21:25 (every man did right in own eyes).

1 Samuel: 2:12-17 (Eli's sons corrupt); 13:14 (David after God's heart).

2 Samuel: 8:17 (Zadok as priest); 15:24-29 (Zadok's loyalty).

1 Chronicles: 6:3-8 (Zadok's lineage); 24:1-19 (priestly courses); 24:10 (Abijah's course); 29:22 (Zadok anointed).

Appendix A: Timeline, High Priests, Glossary, and Scriptural References

2 Chronicles: 30:26 (Hezekiah's Passover joy); 32:20-21 (angel defeats Assyrians).

Psalms: 16 (resurrection); 89:34 (God's unchanging covenant).

Isaiah: 35:1 (desert blossoms); 35:8 (way of holiness); 35:10 (ransomed return); 40:3 (voice in wilderness); 61:1 (Spirit upon Messiah).

Ezekiel: 36:26-27 (new spirit); 36:27 (Spirit within); 44:15-16 (Zadokites keep sanctuary); 44:23 (holy vs. profane).

Daniel: 11:31 (abomination of desolation).

Joel: 2:28-29 (Spirit on all flesh).

Amos: 5:27 (exile beyond Damascus).

Zechariah: 4:14 (two anointed ones); 6:12-13 (Branch builds Temple).

Malachi: 3:1-2 (messenger prepares way); 4:5-6 (Elijah's return).

New Testament (HTV for Matthew; KJV for others)

Matthew (HTV): 1:1-17 (Yeshua's genealogy); 3:2 (repent); 3:4 (John's lifestyle); 3:6 (baptism); 3:7 (vipers); 4:17 (kingdom at hand); 5:17-18 (fill Torah); 11:14 (John as Elias); 15:6 (tradition voids command); 21:12-13 (Temple cleansing); 23:2 (scribes sit in Moses' seat); 23:13 (woe to scribes/Sadducees).

Mark: 1:5 (baptism in Jordan).

Luke: 1:5 (Zacharias' lineage); 1:15-17 (John's spirit of Elias); 1:80 (John in deserts); 4:18 (Spirit upon me).

John: 16:13 (Spirit guides).

Acts: 1:8 (witness to ends of earth); 1:14 (women pray); 2:1-4 (Pentecost); 2:17 (Spirit on all flesh); 2:38 (repent/baptize); 2:41 (3,000 baptized); 2:44-45 (all in common); 3:19 (repent/refreshing); 4:32 (all in common); 5:3-5 (Ananias/Sapphira); 8:3 (Paul persecutes); 9:1-2 (persecutes the Way); 9:3-5 (conversion); 9:17-18 (baptized); 15:20-21 (abstain idols); 18:26 (Priscilla teaches); 22:3 (Paul under Gamaliel).

Romans: 3:31 (establish law); 8:14 (led by Spirit); 15:26 (collection for poor).

1 Corinthians: 5:7-8 (Passover); 12:7-11 (spiritual gifts); 16:1-3 (offerings).

Galatians: 1:17-18 (Arabia/Damascus).

Ephesians: 2:19-20 (household of God).

Colossians: 2:8 (vain deceit).

Hebrews: 7:17 (priest after Melchisedec).

Revelation: 11:3-4 (two witnesses).

Appendix B:
The Ineffable Name of Yehováh

Insert from:
Sons of Zion vs Sons of Greece
Dr. Miles R. Jones (pp. 151-162)

The Ineffable Name of Yehováh

It was not enough to kill Yeshua - the Messiah of Yehovah! The sacred name had to be wiped out lest the power of Yehovah and His Son be greater after martyrdom than before. We are dealing with a conjunction of evil intent committed by Greeks, Romans, Jews and Gentiles that has prevailed now for millennia! The prohibition of the sacred name Yehovah had been attempted by the Greek Emperor Antiochus Epiphanies 200 years before Yeshua - and many of the corrupt Sadducee priests went along with it - interpreting Hebrew Scripture to give cover to this naked grab for power over the Jews' spiritual beliefs. But it outraged the people. Led by the Maccabees, they revolted and - by the hand of Yehovah - liberated themselves from Greek rule! The use of the *'Sacred Name'* became more prevalent than ever.

The Romans were more brutally effective than the Greeks. After the Jewish revolts of 70 and 135 AD, they slaughtered a million and a half Jews, razed the Temple and Jerusalem itself, and forbade the people to even mention the name of Yehovah - upon penalty of death! The Jewish priests eventually made a virtue of necessity and informed the populace the *'Ineffable Name'* of God was too sacred to be pronounced anyway. Only the priests would say *"The Name"* once a year under strict conditions. The constraint followed that *'The Name'* [HaShem] should never be written completely lest one be able to say it. The Menorah was also declared too sacred for Jews to have in their homes, from now on it would only be used in the Temple.

Jewish believers were forbidden to have a Menorah or to pronounce *'The Name.'* Gentile Christians followed in order to change *'The Name'* to Greek. **"The sacred name was stripped from out of the NT and the LXX [Septuagint] versions of the OT by scribes believing in the ineffable name doctrine (a process that began early in the second century C.E.)"**[1] In the 3rd century, Rabbi Hanina used the sacred name of God in his teaching. According to the rabbis, *"It was God who was offended by this and who sentenced Rabbi Hanina to be burned alive at the hand of the Romans."*[2] **Many Jews now believe their salvation will be lost if they utter the sacred name Yehovah!**

Greek Gentile Christians were happy to buy into the *'Ineffable Name.'* They wanted to change the names *'Yehovah'* and *'Yeshua'* to Greek names! They were creating a Greek Church that was soon to divorce itself from the Messianic Church. To do this they needed to be free of any authority the Hebrews might have over them. **The authority of this new Greek Church was deeply vested in the language of Scripture. They needed Greek Scripture, Greek liturgy, a Greek God and a Greek Jesus!**

How well did they succeed? *'Yehovah'* and *'Yeshua'* sound funny and foreign now to contemporary Christians. One might counter that the name is recorded in the Old Testament, cited in its German form *'Jehóvah,'* a name found nowhere in Hebrew. Even so, the 1611 King James Version replaced YHVH with *"LORD"* and that convention was ultimately followed by the Revised Standard Version, New American Bible, New International Version, etc. The sacred name - *Yehováh* - is now *passé* in modern Christianity. Here is the standard explanation:

---

1   R. Clover, 2002:p.158, *The Sacred Name YHVH,* Qadesh La Yahweh Press.
2   Nehemia Gordon, 2012:p.94, *Shattering the Conspiracy of Silence,* Hilkiah.

Appendix B: The Ineffable Name of Yehováh

> *Bibles use "Lord" instead of YHVH or Jehovah because of the practice begun by the Jews hundreds of years before Christ. The Jews did not want to pronounce or mispronounce the name of YHVH out of reverence. They did not want to risk violating the commandment that says,*
>
> *"You shall not take the name of the Lord your God in vain, for the Lord will not leave him unpunished who takes His name in vain."*

So, the Jews began substituting for God's name (in Hebrew, *"Adonai")* which is now *Lord*. This practice is followed today in English translations of the Bible to show reverence for the Holy Name. Finally, since the early Hebrew text did not contain vowels but only consonants, it is not known exactly how to pronounce God's name. So, LORD is substituted for YHVH.[3]

Nowhere in the Bible, New Testament or Old, does it say that the sacred name of God - *Yehováh* - is forbidden! This is a commandment of men! Its erasure is the greatest abomination ever committed!

There are three arguments. **One**, saying the sacred name is forbidden by the third commandment since *"the Lord will not leave him unpunished who takes His name in vain"* (Ex 20:7). **Two**, both Jews and Christians do it out of reverence for the sacred name. **Three**, it is no longer known how to pronounce the sacred name of God anyway, so presumably we can do whatever we wish. In my experience, I have found that church tradition (*"the commandments of men"*) will trump the Word of God almost every time. This is the result of doctrinal programming, peer pressure and the influence of Satan. All three arguments given above fall apart upon examination.

Number One, the sacred name is forbidden by the third

---
3   Mike Slick, 2009, *"Why do Bibles use 'LORD' instead of YHVH,"* carm.org..

commandment so as not to risk taking His name in vain. Note that after Moses revealed the Ten Commandments, the sacred name of Yehovah continued to be invoked in Scripture thousands more times for more than 1000 years. Even the most Greek of Greek theologians, past or present, did not interpret this commandment as a prohibition of the sacred name. It is generally cited as meaning to swear falsely or irreverently by the name of God, cursing His name, or cursing in His name. Those are certainly valid examples but do not convey the most complete meaning of the third commandment.

The literal Hebrew translation of the third commandment is:

> *"You shall not take away the name of Yehovah your Elohim to nothing" (Ex 20:7).*

The more common translation is *"take the name of God in vain."* The name *'Yehovah'* is specifically stated in the third commandment. The word *'shav'* - *'in vain'* means *'to nothing'* or *'naught'* from the root word *'shov'* meaning to desolation, ruin or waste. Naught can also mean false - as lies mean *nothing*. In every usage of the word *'shav'* in the Bible one may substitute *to nothing* or *naught*, such as in Exodus 20:7.[4]

You shall not make the name Yehovah naught!

To prohibit, change or take away the name Yehovah is to render it naught. To erase the name of God - Yehovah - is to make it nothing, even if done with the very best of intentions. Satan revels in deflecting the faith of believers into destruction, ruin and waste. It is his most prized triumph, to misdirect the faith of God's chosen in vain - to nothing - or to a harmful end.

Number Two, both Jews and Christians do it out of reverence for the sacred name. Jewish priests invented the *'Ineffable Name'* doctrine under the boot of - first their Greek tyrants - then their Roman ones. *"The rabbis had to make a choice between losing an entire generation of Jewish leaders or adapting to the Roman*

---

4   See Strong's Concordance - Hebrew word number H7723.

Appendix B: The Ineffable Name of Yehováh

prohibition against speaking God's name."[5] Later generations believed this ban was *'Law.'* Nonetheless, their belief has no support in Scripture!

Christians did not adopt the Ineffable Name doctrine out of reverence for the sacred name. They did so because they wished to change it. A rising tide of anti-Semitism animated the Greeks' separation from the Messianic Church. The Hebrew revolts against the Greeks and Romans were called the *"Messianic Wars"* because every new revolutionary leader was hailed as the conquering-king Messiah.

Judaism in the first century was a powder keg of Messianic fever, boiling under ever more brutal Roman oppression. The Romans feared the new Messianic religion - convinced it would spread revolution throughout the empire. Persecution of the early Church was motivated largely by this fear. Greek believers, suffering mightily under persecution, soon separated themselves from all things Hebraic by creating a Greek religion and ultimately rejecting the Messianic Church.

Number Three, the correct pronunciation of the sacred name of God had been lost - even to the Jews - due to more than two millenia of suppression of the Name. After much research of the Name of God for this book I came to the conclusion that it was *"Yahweh."* Then I heard Nehemia Gordon speak on *"The Name of God"* and within minutes two things changed in my thinking!

My *'conclusion'* about the sacred name *'Yahweh'* lay in tatters - and it became crystal clear the Jews had never lost the pronunciation of the sacred name of God. I made a mistake so fundamental that I am embarrassed to recount it. How ironic that while researching a book insisting we must consider our Hebrew roots - I failed to study any Hebrew sources on the sacred name of God. Nehemia Gordon did and his research, outlined in his

---
5   Nehemia Gordon, 2012:p.96, *Shattering the Conspiracy of Silence*, Hilkiah.

book *Shattering the Conspiracy of Silence*, is definitive!

I had read Nehemia's work and emailed him that I would be at his presentation and hoped to meet with him. We had only a few minutes to speak before and after as he had to leave immediately for an engagement in another city. Two days later I drove to Dallas to have coffee with him. We spoke for five hours on the sacred name of God, the translation of the *Hebrew Gospels from Catalonia*, and the discovery of previously unknown Shem Tov manuscripts that he has pursued for many years. We remain, to the best of my knowledge - one Jew and one Gentile - the only two scholars researching the survival of *The Hebrew Gospels*.

> *"God's name could not have been a secret. The Jewish multitudes heard it ten times every Yom Kippur directly from the mouth of the high priest. They also heard it three times every day from the regular priests pronouncing the Priestly Blessing. If this was a secret it was the worst kept secret in history."*[6]

Although Nehemia Gordon is speaking of the first century, this is an example of how cut off Gentile Bible scholars are from their Hebraic roots. **The sacred Name had not been forgotten**! Even after the Roman ban in the 2nd century, there was a Jewish ritual - every few years teachers would reveal the sacred Name '*Yehováh*' to their disciples.

In the fifth century, Theodoret of Cyprus wrote in Greek the sacred name was '*Yahweh*' based on a Samaritan tradition, hardly a reliable source. Like all Christian scholars - Theodoret did not know Hebrew. As a result of this willful ignorance of Hebrew sources, the Yahweh tradition took hold and grew. The Jews were certainly not going to correct the error. **Christianity had successfully silenced the sacred name of God!**

Was this what Yehovah wanted? Was this all part of his plan to bestow the mantle of the chosen people upon Greek Christianity? Was this a deeper truth that we have uncovered in the fullness of our modern more mature spiritual wisdom? Any pastor

---
[6] Nehemiah Gordon, 2012:p.84, *Shattering the Conspiracy of Silence*, Hilkiah.

who does not agree will likely be forced to give up his clerical credentials, his congregation, his paycheck and membership in his denomination. Without a real and profound desire for truth we are easily deceived!

I pray my readers will become less concerned about offending others and more concerned about offending Yehovah!

Nehemia once said, *"I never met a Jewish rabbi who thought the name was Yahweh!"* Over time as the ban on the sacred name took root, most ordinary Jews no longer knew the pronunciation. However, knowledge of it was never lost to the rabbis and Jewish cognoscenti. In 1225 AD, Eleazar of Worms wrote the *Book of the Divine Name* which described the ceremony by which master teachers could transmit the sacred name Yehovah to their students every seven years. Nehemia cited 14 rabbis giving the pronunciation of Yehovah in writing over the centuries. **The consonants - YHVH - of the sacred Name were, and still are, used in the Hebrew Scripture. Only the vowels were in doubt.**

The Tikkunei Zohar, 1300 AD, gave the vowels of YHVH:

Sometimes the vowels were encoded so as to obscure them from those the Jews felt had no business knowing the sacred name. In 1608, the Shabbethai Sofer said, *"behold, when it is read as YH[VH] in the world to come, then its vowels will be "SHaCHaK."* Within this made-up word are the first letters of the vowels; *SHeva, CHolam, Kamatz.* Yeshayahu Horowitz, in the 17th century, wrote *"it is known that the name YHVH has the vowels... [with the] acronym 'SHaCHaK.'"*

Meir Mahar'am of Lublin, also writing in the 1600s, felt compelled to make it more explicit, *"concerning the vowels of the Tetragrammaton - received from Sinai - which are sheva, cholam, kamatz."* Jacob Bachrach, in 1896, wrote at some length on the sacred Name. He contested the claim YHVH is said to have the vowels of *'Adonai.'* That would make the name *'Yahovaih'*, which is not correct, nor is it found in any version of Scripture. Jacob Bachrach said, ***"the vowels sheva, cholam, kamatz are unique to the sacred name… and are eternal."***[7]

Usually when vowel pointing is used with YHVH, it will leave off the *cholam*, the dot over the middle of the name which is the long 'o' sound. This is done to make it unpronounceable. This transforms it from the three-syllable name *Yehováh* into a two-syllable word *'Yehvah'* often pronounced as *'Yahweh.'* The *Yahweh* pronunciation is not possible within the rules of Hebrew. There are two problems, you cannot have an *'h'* in the middle of a word without a following vowel. We have come across this rule before, on the YHVH stone given to Dr. Kim by the Prince of Mecca. It came from the Saudi Royal Museum collection, originally picked up by Bedouins from Tabuk close to Mount Sinai in Arabia. It had the letters YHVH which the critics claimed were actually WHHY. Such a word cannot be, for Hebrew does not have medial *'h'*s without following vowels.

The second problem is stress. Hebrew words are accented, or stressed, on the last syllable. In English, and various other languages, words are stressed on the second to last syllable. In Hebrew, when unstressed the *Yah* becomes *Yeh*, the /ah/ sound becoming a shorter /eh/ sound. This is apparent from the name *Yeshúa* which comes from the name of God *Yah-shua* (God saves) but it is unstressed in the first syllable which becomes *Ye*. *Yahweh* is not possible in Hebrew. *Yahweh* is a Gentile invention.

Nehemia relates the moment when he discovered the name of God with all the correct vowels written in the Hebrew text of the Bible, as *"something that changed my life."* *"Now that I knew how to pronounce God's name, I was reading it as 'Yehovah'*

[7] 2018, notes taken at Nehemia Gordon's presentation, *'The Name of God.'*

even when it said 'Yehvah' in the manuscript... This must have been what happened to the scribes."[8]

In short, the secret was kept by leaving out the middle vowel, "rarely, less than 1% of the time, they slipped up writing God's name with a full set of vowels." Not only did Nehemia find *Yehovah* with full vowels in the *Biblia Hebraica Stuttgartensia*, but also six times in the *Aleppo Codex*, and when he checked the *Leningrad Codex* - where he was able to do a digital search - he found the sacred name with full vowels dozens of times. Since then, **Gordon has found it in more than 1000 manuscripts, thousands of times! There is no more doubt about the pronunciation of YHVH.**

It is Yehováh!

The YHVH-Ba'al Cult

The disappearance of the sacred name *Yehováh*, in Christian manuscripts, is an absolute abomination! It has happened before, during the YHVH-Baal cult spoken of in Scripture, and God condemned it with a finality that every believer should be aware of. After the Israelites had conquered Canaan and began to mix seed with their much more sophisticated pagan neighbors, they were seduced into pagan worship. The Canaanites offered the ploy 'YHVH=Ba'al - Same=Same.' Baal was just another name for the one supreme God.[9]

King Saul had named his son *"Eshbaal"* or *"Man of Baal."* Even King David was swayed, naming his son *"B'elyada"* which means *"Baal knows."*[10] Those names were changed by the author of the

---

8   Nehemia Gordon, 2012:p.77, *Shattering the Conspiracy of Silence*, Hilkiah.
9   See Strong's Concordance #1167 - Baal as Lord, a deity, master, or husband.
10 I Chronicles 8:33.

book of Samuel to *"Elyada"* - *"God knows"* and *"Ishboshet"* - *"Man of shame"* a reflection of just how badly these two kings had transgressed against the sacred name of God![11] They were not alone. The word *"Baali"* had become a synonym for *"My God - Yehovah."* Yehovah Himself condemned this substitute of the name *Ba'al* for his sacred name:

> *And it shall be at that day, said Yehovah, that you shall call me 'Ishi' [Hebrew for 'my husband' or 'my master']; and shall call me no more 'Ba'ali' ['my husband' or 'my god - Ba'al']*[12] *- Hosea 2:16 [brackets mine]*

It was King Solomon, however, whose *"Ammonite wife convinced him to build the 'Topheth,' an altar for sacrificing children to Molech."*[13] The *Topheth* was a hollow statue of Molech made of iron - placed within a fire pit in the Hinnom Valley just outside of Jerusalem. It was called *Ge-Hinnom,* in Greek *Gehenna,* or as translated into English - *Hell!* The statue would be heated in the fire pit until it was red hot then the sacrificial infant would be placed into the bright red arms of the idol - as flutes and drums made a cacophony to mask the shrieks of the baby being seared to death! **Now you can see the slippery slope of the YHVH-Baal cult! Baal, and Molech, demanded human sacrifice. Yehovah declared it an abomination!**

> **And they built the high places of Ba'al, which are in the Valley of Hinnom, to cause their sons and daughters to pass through the fire unto Molech;** *which I commanded them not... [to] do this abomination... And now therefore, said Yehovah... this city... it shall be delivered into the hand of the king of Babylon by the sword, and by famine, and by pestilence. (Jeremiah 32:35-36)*

Thus did Yehovah visit a hideous judgment upon his chosen people and his chosen city of Zion, because the prophets of Ba'al

---

11   2nd Samuel 2:10.
12   Strong's #1180, Baali - Jehovah.
13   Nehemiah Gordon, 2012:p.153, *Shattering the Conspiracy of Silence,* Hilkiah.

Appendix B: The Ineffable Name of Yehováh

> *"cause my people to forget My name... as their fathers have forgotten My name for Ba'al" (Jer 23:27).*

They turned to the worship of pagan gods and the practice of their abominations. The name '*Yehovah*' itself had a power and a truth His chosen people had turned away from.

> *"Therefore, behold, I, even I, will utterly forget you, and I will forsake you, and the city that I gave you and your fathers, and cast you out of my presence; And I will bring an everlasting reproach upon you, and a perpetual shame, which shall not be forgotten" (Jeremiah 23:39-40).*

Yehovah had been clear,

> *"I am Yehovah, that is My name, and I will not give My glory to another, nor My praise to engraved images" (Isaiah 42:8).*

He had even prohibited the names of '*Ba'alim*' [pagan/foreign gods] to come from their lips (Exodus 23:13 & Hosea 2:17). Yehovah declared to Elijah,

> *"I have left unto me 7000 in Israel, all the knees which have not bowed down unto Ba'al..." (1 Kings 19:18).*

So Yehovah sent Elijah into a battle of names against the priests of Baal. Elijah challenged them to prepare two bullocks for sacrifice and put them on the wood without fire, and

> ***"you call on the name of your gods, and I will call on the name of Yehovah, and the God that answers by fire, let him be God" (1st Kings 18:24).***

The priests of Baal,

> *"called upon the name of Ba'al from morning until noon, saying, O Ba'al hear us! But there was no voice, nor any that answered" (18:26).*

Elijah soaked his offering with water until the trenches around it were full, then he said,

> *"Yehovah Elohim of Abraham, Isaac and Israel, let it be*

> known this day that you are God in Israel... then the fire of Yehovah fell, and consumed the sacrifice" (18:36-8).

And the entire nation of Israel returned to worship of Yehovah! If we reject the Name *Yehováh* - are we rejecting Him? Above All - Your Name!

This must seem silly to some readers who are convinced it is only natural when writing the Scriptures in Greek, or English, to change the name of Yehovah to something more appropriate to the language and culture one is writing for. I can understand that thinking. But it does not really matter what I think! It matters what Yehovah thinks. Let us see what He thinks about His Name.

> *"You have magnified Your Word, above all Your Name!"* **(Psalm 138:2).**

Yehovah commands us in His Word to declare His sacred name - to speak it, sing it, shout it out joyfully, give glory to it, magnify it, worship it, revere the name, love it, give thanks to it, meditate upon it, ask salvation of it, serve it, bless it, bless others in His name, to trust in the name *Yehovah*, and to swear by it

> *"As Yehovah lives!" (Jer 12:16).*

In the poetry of Psalms, *Yehovah* is used more than 700 times to be sung and recited,

> *"My mouth shall speak the praise of Yehovah, and let all flesh bless His sacred name for ever and ever" (Psalm 145:21).*

> *"Yehováh... This is my name forever, and this is my memorial unto all generations" (Ex 3:15).*

David faced the giant Goliath with these words,

> *"You come to me with sword, and spear, and shield; but I come to you in the name of Yehovah" (1 Sam 17:45).*

The name is a weapon against evil.

> *"Everyone who calls on the name of Yehovah shall be saved" (Joel 2:32).*

Appendix B: The Ineffable Name of Yehováh

> *It is a key to our salvation, both spiritual and physical. "In every place where I cause my name to be remembered - I will come to you and bless you" (Ex 20:24).*

> *Yehovah will bless us just for remembering His name! "Declare the name of Yehovah in Zion" (Psalm 102:21).*

'*Yehováh*' is the most important word in Scripture! And Yehovah said of his Word, *"Do not add to nor take away from it"* (Deut 12:32). **What does Yehovah want?** *"To return unto the people a pure language, that they may all call upon the name of Yehovah, to serve Him with one accord"* (Zeph 3:9). **Scripture provides an avalanche of commands on the blessings of declaring the name Yehovah - and that it is not to be changed nor made naught!**

The teachers of Christianity... find it hard to comprehend that **there is a requirement to use the sacred name** because they have ignored the background of the Old Testament and refused to examine the evidence that the sacred name has been stripped out of the New Testament by those anciently adhering to the *'ineffable name'* doctrine.[14]

Read the prophecy in Psalms,

> *"I will declare your name to my brethren" (Psalm 22:22).*

In the 17th chapter of John, **Yeshua said,**

> *"**I have manifested your name** unto the men you have given me (17:6)... **through your own name** keep those whom you have given me"(17:11)... **I have declared unto them your name - and will declare it!**" (John 17:26).*

This is the weak link in Greek primacy - neither Yeshua nor his Apostles would ever substitute the name of a Greek god for the name of Yehovah! Yehovah has been erased from the

---
14 R. Clover, 2002:p.215, *The Sacred Name YHVH*, Qadesh Yahweh Press.

New Testament, even in quotations from the Old Testament, and by now it has been erased completely from the vast majority of Christian Bibles!

Many Christians condemn all Jews for breaking God's Covenant, yet - although it goes unspoken - the sacred name Yehovah is written in Hebrew Scripture 6957 times. In modern Christian Bibles it does not appear at all. If the Jews have broken the Covenant then Christians have done worse - erased the sacred name of Yehovah from the Covenant contract itself! *"It became official Christian dogma at the beginning of the fourth century when the Roman Church was founded under Constantine. From this point on it was considered 'Jewish' to use the Sacred name."* **It branded one as a *'Judaizer'* - and the penalty for *'Judaizing'* was death!**

The justification I hear most often about the sacred name *'Yehovah'* and why it is not used by Christians, is that, *'God knows my heart.'* This is a paraphrase of Psalm 44:20-21,

"If we have forgotten the name of our God, or stretched out our hands to a strange god: Shall not God search this out? For he knows the secrets of the heart."

The Psalms were written by King David who named one of his sons after Baal. His son, Solomon, revived the YHWH-Ba'al cult, allowing Israelites to burn their babies alive in the Topeth, to appease Baal and Molech!

According to Jeremiah (Jer 7:31), at the very peak of the Israelites' power and prosperity - Yehovah judged them,

"I will forsake you... cast you out of my presence; and I will bring an everlasting reproach upon you, and a perpetual shame, which shall not be forgotten" (Jer 23:40).

Yehovah condemned them to be conquered *"by sword, and by famine, and by pestilence"* (Jer 32:36) for their abominations and because they *"have forgotten my name for Ba'al."* **If you forget His name - declared thousands of times - forgetting His Word and His commandments are sure to follow!**

Appendix B: The Ineffable Name of Yehováh

> *"Make no mention of the name of other gods, neither let it be heard out of your mouth" (Ex 23:13).*

The 44th Psalm, *"For he knows the secrets of the heart"* was not a promise of forgiveness by Yehovah - it was part of a profound condemnation! It was a desperate prayer by the Israelites for mercy! *"You have cast off and put us to shame"* (44:9), *"Awake, why do you sleep, O Yehovah? Arise, cast us not off forever"* (44:23). They pleaded, they had the best of intentions, *"All this is come upon us, yet have we not forgotten you, nor dealt falsely with your covenant"* (44:17). The 44th Psalm was not a promise of forgiveness - quite the opposite.

> *"If we have stretched out our hands to a strange god: Shall not God search this out?* **For he knows the secrets of the heart"** **(Psalm 44:20-21).**

Yehovah did know the secrets of their hearts - and He found them profoundly lacking - and He sent a disastrous judgement upon them!

Nor should one think foreigners are in any way exempted,

> *"Also the sons of foreigners, join themselves to Yehovah, to serve him, to love the name Yehovah" (Isaiah 56:6).*

There is an ancient Hebrew proverb which states, *"An honest man may be mistaken - but once shown the truth - he either ceases to be mistaken, or he ceases to be honest."* Do we wish to know the truth? If so then once it is revealed we move up to a higher level of accountability. Or as Yeshua put it,

> *"If I had not come and spoken unto them, they had no sin: but now they have no cloak for their sin" (John 15:22).*

It is not mine to know the final judgment of Yehovah upon either Christians or Jews but there is one thing I do know - and I know it so deep in my bones that it is unshakeable...

There will be a judgment!

In the Cochin manuscript of Revelation 1:8, we see:

The classic formulation of Yehováh's name which comes from the Hebrew verb "to be."

יְהוָה	הָיָה	הֹוֶה	יִהְיֶה
Yehováh	Who was	Who is	Who will be

The name of Yehováh and His son Yeshua are both subjects of debate. The publication of the *Hebrew Book of Revelation* along with related research on the sacred Names should resolve that debate. Below are displayed the appearance of **the Sacred Name of Yehováh with correct vowel markings in ten manuscripts of *The Hebrew New Testament*!** It demonstrates the Messianic (Jewish-Christian) assemblies' desire to preserve and sanctify the true Name of Yehováh as directed by Yeshua in *The Hebrew Gospels* in John 17:6-26:

> "I have manifested Your Name unto the men you have given me. I have declared unto them Your Name - and I will declare it!"

This was fulfillment of the prophecy in Psalms 22:22,

> "I will declare Your Name to my brethren!"

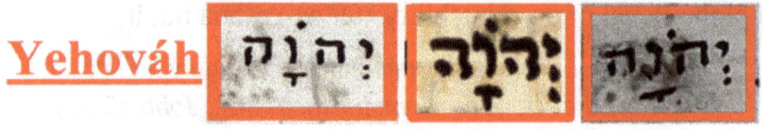

Thanks to Janice Baca for much of the work done on the Name of God.

Some Messianic scribes of *The Hebrew Gospels* continued to use substitute names for Yehovah as they had been instructed in their Hebrew yeshivas (schools). Having recovered four dozen manuscripts of all or part of *The Hebrew Gospels*, it is safe to say that many, if not most, Messianic scribes courageously held to the Sacred Name *Yehováh* with the correct vowel pointing - despite

Appendix B: The Ineffable Name of Yehováh

it being banned by both the Judaic Church and the Greco-Roman Christian Church! By now, thanks to the work of Nehemia Gordon in the Old Testament and my own research in the New Testament - there should be no more question. Unfortunately, ingrained views on this heated debate do not often go away with the mere discovery of evidence. It has become an article of faith to many. Sooner or later, it will sort itself out. The evidence is definitive. Dr. Gordon has now discovered the Name of *Yehováh* with correct vowels in hundreds of manuscripts, thousands of times. I do not know of any instance of *Yahweh* with vowel pointing.

The debate also revolves around the correct given name of *Yeshua*, in Hebrew. Many scribes used the short (Aramaic) version *Yeshu*, while others attached the shortened root form of Yehovah's name *Yah*, or *Yahu*. This renders a variant name for Yeshua -*Yehoshua*. Some have even used the Grecian form of the name Yeshua with a final Greek /s/- *Yeshuas*. Here is the breakdown of their usage in Hebrew texts:

Freiburg 314, Neofiti 33, Augsburg, Yeates,Uppsala 31, Uppsala 32, Add.170, Shepreve 16.A.II, 2 Peter British Library, Vat Ebr 530, Udine Ebr 3, Marsaille MS 24-25	**Yeshua** used in 12 of 20 = **60%** manuscripts	יֵשׁוּעַ
Shem Tov Vat Ebr 101, Cambridge Oo.1.32, Guenzburg 363, Cambridge Oo.1.16.2, Matthew Russia Ms D101	**Yeshu** used in 5 of 20 mss = **25%**	יֵשׁוּ יֵשׁוּ
Sloane Hazon 273, Paris 131	**Yehoshua** used in 2 of 20 mss = **10%**	יְהוֹשֻׁעַ
HGC Vat Ebr 100	**Yeshuas** used in 1 of 20 mss = **5%**	שׁוּאשׁ

Bibliography

Primary Sources

The Holy Bible, King James Version (KJV). Cambridge: Cambridge University Press, 1611.

The Hebrew Book of Matthew: The Original Gospel, Hebrew Text Version (HTV), Great Publishing Company, Benai Emunah Institute, Hebrew Gospels Project, 2025.

Dead Sea Scrolls

Abegg, Martin, Jr., Peter Flint, and Eugene Ulrich, trans. *The Dead Sea Scrolls Bible*. New York: Harper Collins Publishers, 1999.

Vermes, Geza, trans. *The Complete Dead Sea Scrolls in English*. Revised ed. London: Penguin Books, 2004.
> Includes translations of the *Calendrical Texts* (4Q320-321), *Community Rule* (1QS), *Damascus Document* (CD), and *War Scroll* (1QM).

Historical and Classical Texts

Josephus, Flavius. *The Antiquities of the Jews*. Translated by William Whiston. London: William Bohn, 1737.
> References to Essene communities and Jewish sects in the 1st century AD.

Maccabees, 1 and 2. In *The Apocrypha*, edited by Edgar J. Goodspeed. New York: Random House, 1959.
> Historical accounts of the Maccabean revolt and Zadokite exile (e.g., 2 Maccabees 2:4-8).

Secondary Sources

Allegro, John M. *The Dead Sea Scrolls and the Origins of Christianity*. New York: Criterion Books, 1957.

Allegro, John M. *The Dead Sea Scrolls and the Christian Myth*. Amherst, NY: Prometheus Books, 1992.

Baigent, Michael, and Richard Leigh. *Dead Sea Scrolls Deception*. New York: Simon & Schuster, 1993.

Bishop, Bill, and Karen Bishop. *Biblical Calendar Then and Now: Comparing and Contrasting Holy Scripture to the DSS*. Livermore, CA: Wing Span Press, 2018.

Burrows, Millar. *More Light on The Dead Sea Scrolls*. London: Secker & Warburg LTD, 1958.

Campbell, Jonathan. *Deciphering the Dead Sea Scrolls*. London: Fontana Press - Harper Collins, 1996.

Charles, R. H., ed. *The Apocrypha and Pseudepigrapha of the Old Testament in English*. Oxford: Clarendon Press, 1913.

Cross, Frank Moore. *The Ancient Library of Qumran*. 3rd ed. Minneapolis, MN: Fortress Press, 1995.

Danielou, Jean. *Dead Sea Scrolls & Primitive Christianity*. Translated from the French *Manuscrits de la Mer Morte*. Baltimore, MD: Guramond Press, 1958.

Davies, Philip R. *The Damascus Covenant: An Interpretation of the "Damascus Document"*. Sheffield: JSOT Press, 1982.

Driver, G. R. *The Judaean Scrolls*. New York: Schocken Books, 1965.

Driver, G. R. *The Judean Scrolls*. Baltimore, MD: Guramond Press, 1958.

Ehrman, Bart. *Jesus Before the Gospels*. New York: Harper Collins Publishers, 2016.

Eisenman, Robert. *Maccabees, Zadokites, Christians and Qumran: New Hypothesis of Qumran Origins*. Nashville, TN: Grave Distractions Publications, 2013. First published 1986.

Eisenman, Robert, and M. Wise. *The Dead Sea Scrolls Uncovered*. New York: Barnes & Noble Books, 1992.

Eisenman, Robert. *Dead Sea Scrolls and the First Christians*. Coppell, TX: The Way Publishing, 2019. First published 1996.

Eisenman, Robert. *James the Brother of Jesus & the Dead Sea Scrolls*. Vol. 1, *Historical James, Paul the Enemy, & Jesus' Brothers as Apostles*. Coppell, TX: The Way Publishing, 2019. First published 2012.

Eisenman, Robert. *James the Brother of Jesus & the Dead Sea Scrolls*. Vol. 2, *Damascus Code, Tent of David, New Covenant, Blood of Christ*. Coppell, TX: The Way Publishing, 2019. First published 2012.

Eshel, Hanan. *The Dead Sea Scrolls and the Hasmonean State*. Jerusalem: Eerdmans Publishing Company, 2008.

Flusser, David. *The Spiritual History of the Dead Sea Sect*. Tel-Aviv: MOD Books, 1989.

Hanson, Kenneth. *Dead Sea Scrolls: The Untold Story*. Chicago: Council Oaks Books, 1996.

Jones, Miles. *Sons of Zion vs Sons of Greece*. Great Publishing Company, Benai Emunah Institute, 2021.
> The author's foundational work on Zadokite heritage, Essene beliefs, and their influence on early Christianity.

Martinez, Florentino Garcia. *The Dead Sea Scrolls: Qumran Texts in English*. Leiden: E. J. Brill; Grand Rapids, MI: Eerdmans, 1996.

McNamer, Elizabeth, and Bargil Pixner. *Jesus and First-Century Christianity in Jerusalem*. New York/NJ: Paulist Press, n.d.

Mitchell, David. *Messiah ben Joseph*. Glasgow, Scotland: Campbell Publishers, 2023. First published 2016.

Mitchell, David. *Jesus: The Incarnation of the Word*. Glasgow, Scotland: Campbell Publishers, 2021.

Nodet, Etienne, and Justin Taylor. *The Origins of Christianity: An Exploration*. Collegeville, MN: The Liturgical Press, 1998.

Piotrkowski, Meron M. *Priests in Exile: History of the Temple of Onias*. Berlin: De Gruyter Press, 2019.

Rowley, H. H. *The Zadokite Fragments and the Dead Sea Scrolls*. London: SPCK, 1952.

Roth, Cecil. *The Historical Background of the Dead Sea Scrolls*. New York: Philosophical Library, 1959.

Schonfield, Hugh. *The Passover Plot*. London: Hugh & Helene Schonfield World Trust, 1965.

Shanks, Hershel. *Understanding the Dead Sea Scrolls*. New York: Random House, 1992.

Talmon, Shemaryahu. *The World of Qumran from Within*. Jerusalem: Magnes Press - Jerusalem University, 1989.

Thomas Davis, Michael, and Brent Strawn. *Qumran Studies: New Approaches*. Cambridge, UK: Eerdmans Publishing, n.d.

Wacholder, Ben Zion, and Martin G. Abegg. *A Preliminary Edition of the Unpublished Dead Sea Scrolls*. Washington, D.C.: Biblical Archaeology Society, 1991.

Journal Articles

Murphy-O'Connor, J. "An Essene Missionary Document? CD II, 14–VI, 1." *Revue Biblique* 77 (1970): 201–29.
> Examination of the Damascus Document's missionary context.

Online Resources

BiblicalTraining.org. "Zadokite Fragments." Accessed August 24, 2025. https://www.biblicaltraining.org.
> Overview of Zadokite texts and their historical significance.

JewishVirtualLibrary.org. "The Book of Covenant of Damascus." Accessed August 24, 2025. https://www.jewishvirtuallibrary.org.
> Historical background on the Damascus Document and Qumran.

Video Study Series

Jones, Miles. *The Mystery of the First 3000*, Writing Of God, Benai Emunah Institute, 2025.
> The author's 7-Part Video Teaching Series with Eddie Chumney

Jones, Miles. *The Secrets of the Gold Book*, Writing Of God, Benai Emunah Institute, 2025.
> The author's 4-Part Video Teaching Series with Jonathan Felt

Jones, Miles. *What is Yehovah's Calendar?* Writing Of God, Benai Emunah Institute, 2024.
> The author's 5-Part Video Teaching Series

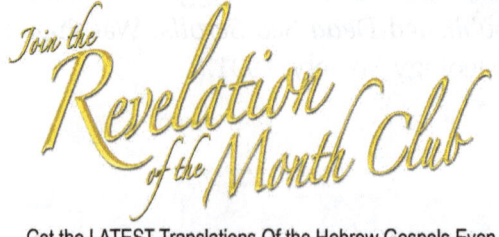

Get the LATEST Translations Of the Hebrew Gospels Even Before they are published - Plus Other Exciting Bonuses

FREE Exerpts from The Unveiled

FREE See the comparison from 4 separate manuscripts depicting the sacred setting of Acts 2.

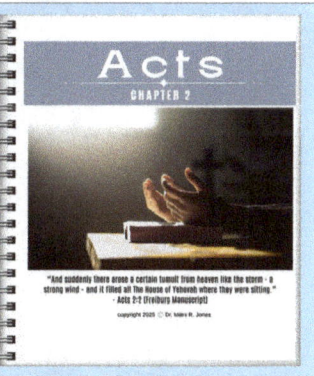

FREE Psalm 24 Audo & Video Files

www.ingramcontent.com/pod-product-compliance
Lightning Source LLC
Chambersburg PA
CBHW050553160426
43199CB00015B/2645